D0391068

The Hidden Gospel of Matthew

Other books in the
SkyLight Illuminations Series

The Hidden Gospel of Matthew

Annotated & Explained

Translation & Annotation
by Ron Miller

Walking Together, Finding the Way
SKYLIGHT PATHS Publishing
Woodstock, Vermont

DISCARD

The Hidden Gospel of Matthew:
Annotated & Explained

2004 First Printing

Translation, annotation, and introductory material © 2004 by Ron Miller

All rights reserved. No part of this book may be reproduced or transmitted in any form or by any means, electronic or mechanical, including photocopying, recording, or by any information storage and retrieval system, without permission in writing from the publisher.

For information regarding permission to reprint material from this book, please mail or fax your request in writing to SkyLight Paths Publishing, Permissions Department, at the address / fax number listed below, or e-mail your request to permissions@skylightpaths.com.

Library of Congress Cataloging-in-Publication Data

Bible. N.T. Matthew. English. Miller. 2004.
The hidden Gospel of Matthew : annotated & explained / translation & annotation by Ron Miller.
        p. cm.—(SkyLight Illuminations series)
Includes bibliographical references.
ISBN 1-59473-038-5
1. Bible. N.T. Matthew—Criticism, interpretation, etc. I. Miller, Ron, 1938– II. Title. III. SkyLight illuminations.
BS2573 2004
226.2'05209—dc22

                                        2004011174

10 9 8 7 6 5 4 3 2 1

Manufactured in the United States of America
Cover Design: Walter C. Bumford III
Cover Art: Portrait of a Man. Roman period, ca. 165 A.D. Encaustic on limewood. ECM 1473. Reproduced by permission of the Provost and Fellows of Eton College.

> SkyLight Paths Publishing is creating a place where people of different spiritual traditions come together for challenge and inspiration, a place where we can help each other understand the mystery that lies at the heart of our existence.
>
> SkyLight Paths sees both believers and seekers as a community that increasingly transcends traditional boundaries of religion and denomination—people wanting to learn from each other, *walking together, finding the way.*

SkyLight Paths, "Walking Together, Finding the Way," and colophon are trademarks of LongHill Partners, Inc., registered in the U.S. Patent and Trademark Office.

Walking Together, Finding the Way
Published by SkyLight Paths Publishing
A Division of LongHill Partners, Inc.
Sunset Farm Offices, Route 4, P.O. Box 237
Woodstock, VT 05091
Tel: (802) 457-4000   Fax: (802) 457-4004
www.skylightpaths.com

To Jim and Carrie
with love
and gratitude

Contents □

Introduction ☐

A Hidden Gospel

There are two ways that a gospel can be hidden. The first is like the Gospel of Thomas, buried in the sands of Egypt for many years. The second is like a manuscript whited over so that a second document can be written on the parchment, or like a picture covered with paint so that the canvas can be used again for a second picture. The technical term for this is *palimpsest,* coming from two Greek words meaning "rubbed smooth" and "again."

The gospel we shall be examining was not buried in the desert like the Gospel of Thomas but lies hidden under the layers of the gospel we call Matthew. The hidden gospel indicates the authentic message of the Teacher from Nazareth before the overlay of later traditions that were edited into the present form of Matthew's gospel. Finding the hidden gospel of Matthew entails painstakingly removing the later layers of tradition so that the original message is disclosed.

This text contains more of the teachings attributed to Jesus than any other document and is thus a primary doorway to Jesus's message, a message needing to be mined in the stone quarry of accumulated layers of Christian tradition found in the text of Matthew. It is a difficult and challenging enterprise but well worth the effort. Our post-9/11 world cries out for the wisdom of Jesus's message.

Reading Sacred Texts

People read sacred texts in radically different ways. This applies not only to atheists, Jews, and Hindus but to Christians as well, in all their denominational varieties. As a matter of fact, the way a Christian approaches the biblical text reveals more about that person's kind of faith and religious understanding than any denominational label. Christians within the same denomination, even the same local church, often read the Bible from radically different perspectives. Conflict about how to see and read the Bible might well be the single greatest issue dividing Christians today.

Conservative Protestant Christians (both the more moderate evangelical Christians and the more extreme fundamentalists) use "biblical inerrancy" as their axiom in reading the Christian Testament. They use the word *true* univocally (i.e., with only one meaning) and thus consider the biblical text true in every respect. They tend to believe that truth about the age of the planet can be found in the Bible just as much as truth about God. The rest of their theology follows as corollaries from that axiom. Using this premise of biblical inerrancy, they achieve an external authority that offers them a secure foothold of belief. Axioms, of course, are not proved, but evangelical and fundamentalist Christians believe that the biblical text itself confirms their starting point—a process that strikes outsiders as a cyclical form of reasoning.

Conservative Roman Catholic Christians find their axiom in an "infallible magisterium," which indicates the authoritative teaching role of church officials, especially the pope. Again, although an axiom cannot strictly be proved, evidence for adherents of this position is found both in the scriptural claim (Matthew 16:18) that Jesus founded his church on Peter and in the perseverance of this church, understood as Peter's bark, through the storms of history. Here too an external authority offers security to the church member who might otherwise flounder.

Rationalists read the text within the parameters of the empirical sciences and what they consider to be the right use of reason. Such readers may think of themselves as atheists or humanists, as Christians or as members of another faith. What they share in common is their assumption that anything that does not fit the criteria of the current scientific consensus must be rejected. The scientific methodology itself provides their ultimate axiom, and they are unwilling to stray beyond its conclusions. Texts are pared down to a residue that seems compatible with "reason," a term usually understood as synonymous with the current scientific worldview.

Comfortable with none of these three approaches, others (Christians and non-Christians alike) come to these texts from a vantage point that I term *transformational*. Representing my own approach to the material, the axiom in this instance is human experience, understanding that experience in the broadest context possible. In other words, truth claims must somehow ring true with one's own sense of life and the kind of growth one is seeking for oneself and one's society.

Approaching Matthew's gospel as a path of personal and societal transformation opens up a new form of inquiry. We find in the text truths consonant with our deepest human experience. We see there possibilities for the transformation of individuals and societies. The axiom of human experience in its potential for transformation, like all the others, cannot be proved; but I find in this premise the most fruitful way of encountering a text.

Faith and Interfaith

The formal teachings of the world's religions often differ from one another. In this world of multiple religious truths, we cannot expect to find identity in religious language. And yet, diverse verbal formulations may serve as signposts pointing to the same mystery, the same divine center. This enables us to regard the world's many sacred traditions as allies, often sharing common teachings as well as similar forms of practice. Meditation and prayer, the attention to consciousness, the diminution of ego, a commitment to compassion and social justice—these and numerous other characteristics serve to unite the practitioners of the world's major sacred traditions.

The literal meaning of *inspire* is to "breathe into," and the transformational approach readily accepts sacred texts as thus inspired by the Divine Spirit. But such inspiration in no way denies the many errors of thought and expression found in the text. In other words, we approach the text in search of its transformational meaning, not expecting insights or information regarding biology or history. The language of Matthew's gospel remains partial, particular, interpreted, and imperfect like all human language, including my own. But I nevertheless find in this less-than-perfect language a hint and shadow of a transcending mystery, a path up the mountain, a spoke connecting me and every reader of this gospel to a common hub, something that no more bears the label "Christian" than it does the label "Jewish" or "Buddhist."

Two Different Christian Perspectives

For Paul, the atoning death of Jesus and his subsequent resurrection constitute the main themes of his gospel; the teachings of Jesus play a secondary role for him and are rarely cited in the extensive corpus of his letters. For Matthew, the source of the largest body of materials attributed to Jesus, the opposite seems to be the case. Jesus's teachings, constituting the new messianic Torah, seem to lie at the heart of Matthew's gospel, while the story of the death and resurrection of Jesus are secondary. Matthew's gospel, nevertheless, lies partially under the wing of Pauline theology in this regard, whereas there are other ancient sources—especially the Letter of James, the Didache, and the Gospel of Thomas—that seem to downplay the centrality of the death and resurrection story even further or ignore it altogether.

An atoning death makes sense only where there is need for atonement. For Paul, the sin of Adam must be atoned for by the sacrifice of the new Adam. In other words, the concept of an atoning death appears in tandem with the idea of original sin. Nothing in the teaching of Jesus talks about this fundamental alienation from God, which looms so large for Paul. Jesus knows about sins, but like most Jews, he regards them as thoughts, words, or deeds that miss the mark of the divine will.

If you have been immersed in the teachings of Jesus and then read the first few chapters of Paul's letter to the Romans, the change of theological worldview will shock you like a plunge into Lake Michigan on a cold January day. For Paul, there are sins, but there is also Sin. The primordial disobedience of the first human couple totally destroyed our capacity to relate to God. Paul sees more than the human proclivity to "miss the mark," the *yetzer ha ra* (evil inclination) acknowledged by rabbinic thought. Paul sees a human nature so thoroughly destroyed through the primordial sin of our first parents that the present world order is controlled by cosmic forces of evil. The result of this dismal picture is that human beings need an external redeemer to be delivered from this condition.

In other words, if the human condition appears helpless, the intervention by God is paramount, and an atoning death seems necessary. If, on the other hand, human nature remains robust, capable of responding to the divine invitation, then the teachings of Jesus will be of more importance than any interpretation of his death. Paul opts for the former scenario; Matthew leans toward the latter, though not as wholeheartedly as some of the other early sources cited.

Jesus as Teacher Rather Than as Redeemer

Since my own theology eschews any teaching of an original sin that totally destroys our ability to respond to the divine call, I lean more toward Matthew's presentation than Paul's, though I am even closer to the Gospel of Thomas than to Matthew. This means that the metaphor of Jesus's death as an atoning sacrifice plays a minimal role in my conception of Christianity. More important is our ability to respond to Jesus's teachings and thus move toward the divine center that constitutes our own inmost reality. The pivot of this discussion lies with whether or not we see the transformation of death to life primarily in Jesus's death and resurrection or in his life and teaching.

The Gospel of Thomas, which makes no mention of Jesus's death or resurrection in its 114 sayings, assures us in its opening words that whoever understands these teachings will have eternal life. Because I find this approach to Jesus and thus to Christianity more persuasive than the metaphor of an atoning death with the theological baggage it necessarily carries, the whole story of the death and resurrection functions more as an addendum for me than as the central message of the gospel. I am sure this will remain an issue of debate among Christians for some time, since both sides recognize its potential for influencing and eventually judging the forms of Christianity emerging in this new millennium. In other words, there are not only individual Christians but whole communities of Christians whose understanding of Jesus and the Christian life match more closely the teachings of Thomas than those of Paul.

Historical Jesus and Christ of Faith

The historical Jesus and the Christ of faith are most frequently exhibited as rivals. It often seems as though we must choose sides, pitting one against the other. When we speak of the Christ of faith, we are no longer operating within the limits of historical methodology. What we say about the Christ of faith has more to do with participating in mystery than with problem solving. When I assert, for example, that Joe is six feet tall, that is something you can prove; but when I claim that Joe is my friend, I have asserted something not empirically verifiable. I have moved from the realm of problem to the realm of mystery. One can walk around the world forever with a yardstick, but it will never disclose the measure of a friend.

When one asserts that Jesus spent most of his public ministry in the Galilee, that postulates a truth that historians of any persuasion can include in their consensus paper. To claim that Jesus was thought to be a healer might also find a consensus. But to say that Jesus healed by the power of God is a statement that goes beyond the canons of historical study. This does not mean that it is not true; it simply means that it is not true according to the canons of contemporary historical writing. Why not? Because there are other explanations. The purported healings might have been cases of spontaneous remission, or they might have involved magic or the invocation of demonic powers. That a particular statement does not belong in the historical consensus does not mean that it is not true; it simply means that it cannot be established as true the way historians use that word.

Since my primary approach is in terms of spiritual transformation, I shall employ the methods of history, but I shall not restrict myself to those methods. In many instances, I shall respond to the text in terms of my own participation in the mystery of Jesus. I shall, in other words, often speak from my personal faith. For I believe that it is only by acknowledging the perspective of faith that we can tap the potential spirituality residing in the text, as well as in the person who is both disclosed and hidden there.

Acknowledgments

I want to thank Lake Forest College for giving me the support system I needed for my research. Student assistants have contributed significantly to this project during the past several years, especially Ed Wingenbach, Matt Sauer, Alison Freund, Shannon Neal, Rick Smith, Amanda Hays, Chris Eichmann, Lisa Wagner, Matt Patterson, and Adriana Wojcik. In several semesters, my entire class on "The Historical Jesus" read the developing manuscript and helped me to make some needed corrections. Some recent alumni of the college—especially Rory McEntee, Brennan Young, and James Klasen—have also been kind enough to read the manuscript and suggest revisions, as have my friends and colleagues Laura Bernstein, Adriana Rosado-Bonewitz, and Priscilla Rockwell. Another recent alumnus and friend, Travis Moran, made editorial corrections to the text. Our department secretary, Andrea Muench, and our student workers fit the manuscript to the publication guidelines. The help of all of these good people has been crucial at every step, and their camaraderie has brightened the path of learning we walk together. I also want to thank Common Ground, an adult center of interfaith study and dialogue in the greater Chicago area, for the opportunity to teach a three-year class on Matthew's gospel, the starting point for much of what is presented here. This book would not have been published without the intervention of

Wayne Teasdale, who introduced me to Jon Sweeney of SkyLight Paths Publishing, and I am grateful to both of them. Finally, I want to thank my children, Jim and Carrie, not only for the technical help they gave me but, more important, for their personal support and love during a difficult transition in my life. This book is dedicated to them.

A New Look at an Old Text ☐

Bringing Out Old and New Treasures

Honored as the first of the twenty-seven books of the Christian Testament, Matthew's gospel gives us an ecclesiastically approved version of the Christian message. It challenges us, therefore, to build a bridge from a thought milieu of two thousand years in the past to our present world of lived experience. Many of the premises of Matthew's world are foreign to us—a heaven above and a hell below, hostile demons, a persecuted Christian minority, a powerful Roman Empire, an unbelieving Jewish world, and an imminent end of the present world order.

There are numerous scholarly commentaries on Matthew's gospel, just as there is an abundance of devotional literature and sermonic material on its every chapter and verse. Many scholars feel that in Matthew 13:52 one of the authors of this text refers to himself when he writes: "Every Torah scholar, then, who becomes a disciple of God's reign is like a rich homeowner who goes into his storage room and brings out both old and new treasures." This primary author was a Torah scholar (i.e., a student of the core of Jewish teaching, the first five books of the Bible: Genesis, Exodus, Leviticus, Numbers, and Deuteronomy) who, upon joining the new Jesus movement, saw himself as bringing out both old and new treasures in his gospel. Our goal is the same: to bring out the old treasure of Matthew's story and the new treasure of a rediscovered Jesus that is meaningful for our experience today.

Which Matthew Are We Talking About?

When the text refers to Matthew, we're usually talking about the canonical gospel we find in the Christian Testament. Because this text has multiple sources, various editors contributed to its completed form. Using a scholarly shorthand, writers will also sometimes speak of Matthew as the corporate persona for all those who had a hand in writing this text. This will include, but not be limited to, the Jewish scribe whose work is prominent in this text. For the sake of convenience, we will refer to him as Matthew, too. Finally, there is the man in this gospel identified as Matthew the tax-collector. There's no assurance that he had any influence on the composition of this gospel. The context should make it clear which Matthew is being talked about in any given sentence.

The Pieces Making the Whole

Although there are contrary scholarly opinions, a certain consensus exists among the critical students of this text. Matthew and Luke were written after Mark, both using Mark as one of their sources. We find, for example, over 600 of Mark's 652 verses in Matthew. One way I try to gain some insight into Matthew is to look over his shoulders, so to speak, seeing how he changes Mark's text and adapts it to his own purposes. Sometimes he drops things that he obviously finds embarrassing; at other times he changes things he finds confusing; and yet again he expands things to include elements that he feels need to be said.

In addition to Mark, Matthew shares another source with Luke, although this source is not extant and available as is Mark. There are some 225 verses where Matthew and Luke agree but that have no parallel in Mark. The material shared in these cases tends to be teaching material, not narrative. Scholars formed two hypotheses from this evidence: (1) the gospels were probably preceded by collections of Jesus's sayings (first in the original Aramaic that Jesus spoke and then in a Greek translation); (2) one such list of sayings, shared by Matthew and Luke, explains their agreement in the 225 verses not found in Mark. The German scholars spearheading this research called this unnamed source Q from the German word *Quelle*, which simply means "source."

In addition to Mark and Q, some materials in this gospel are found only in Matthew. Scholars term this source Special Matthew. Matthew, then, wrote his text with three sources in front of him: Mark, Q, and Special Matthew. These terms will be employed in discussions of the text of Matthew. My goal, however, is not to focus on these terms and distinctions (there are numerous studies that do that) but to touch on them only insofar as they serve our purposes: the disclosure of the historical Jesus, his teachings, and the relationship of those teachings to our experienced world. In other words, we are seeking the gospel hidden under these layers of editing.

Matthew as Midrash

The extensive time I have spent with Matthew's gospel in recent years has impressed me with new images of this ancient writing. As a young reader of the text I saw it primarily as a biography of Jesus, written in all likelihood by an eyewitness. Scholars, however, find in the gospel a carefully crafted proclamation of faith, developed in a community of Jesus believers from both Jewish and Gentile backgrounds, sometime toward the end of the first century C.E. The author of the gospel was probably a Jewish Torah scholar or scribe who at some point joined this community and eventually came to articulate its faith. The gospel both confirms the faith of Matthew's associates and serves as an overture to the larger Jewish and Gentile worlds, presenting itself as an authoritative interpretation of God's dealings with humankind at this juncture of history, a bridge from the Torah of Moses to the Torah of the Messiah.

Midrash is the Hebrew term for commentary, the accumulated insights that interpret not only what is said in the text of the Hebrew Bible but what is unsaid—not only the words used but the number of times they are used. Furthermore, since every Hebrew letter has a numerical equivalent as well, every Hebrew word is also a mathematical sum. This means that some forms of midrash involve the numbers contained in the very letters of the Hebrew text.

Matthew's gospel uses all of these forms of midrash. Furthermore, he weaves more than one hundred direct quotes from the Hebrew Bible (what some Christians call the Old Testament) into his narrative. No wonder commentators consistently remind us that there exists no better background for the study of Matthew's gospel than the Jewish scriptures, for the major figures in the Hebrew Bible, its theological concepts, its very phrases and words—these provide the basic colors that Matthew uses to paint his picture of Jesus and his message.

Once I had the privilege of teaching the Christian Testament as an ongoing two-year adult education workshop at a nearby synagogue. I was struck by the fact that this Jewish audience was more informed about and aware of many of the key issues than the average Christian group. This follows from the simple awareness of how vitally the Hebrew Bible lives in every verse of the Christian Testament. Furthermore, any serious student of the text soon comes to realize that not one major theological concept in the gospels originates outside the Hebrew Bible. Monotheism, creation, sin, repentance, Messiah, vicarious suffering, sacrifice, commandments, God's reign, resurrection, and the final judgment at the close of human history—all of these are as Jewish as they are Christian.

The very structure of Matthew's text reflects a pattern inherited from the Hebrew Bible, namely, five books of teaching paralleling the five books of the Torah. Figures like Abraham, Moses, David, Elijah, the suffering servant of Second Isaiah, and Jeremiah appear in the text through either direct reference or indirect allusion. Some scholars are convinced that a great deal of what seems to be history in these gospels actually falls into the category of prophecy historicized. In other words, the gospel writer starts with a prophecy in the Hebrew Bible and then weaves that prophecy into his narrative account of Jesus's life. This offers but one more example of Matthew's penchant for midrash.

Matthew as a "New and Enhanced Version" of Mark

What should be clear from this discussion of multiple sources is that this gospel arises from a relatively long and complex editorial history. Materials continued to be added, and the final editing probably took place around 85 C.E. Since no extant copy of the text can be dated earlier than the second century, other editorial hands may have made further changes in those next hundred years. This means that what we have in our hands is a much-edited document. The gospel offers a portrait of Jesus, not a photograph. Its organization is more theological than chronological. It progressively introduces the reader to the mystery of Jesus the Messiah: first as healer and teacher, later as one who transforms death into life, suffering into salvation.

Why did Matthew first choose to enhance Mark? Because Matthew, like the other gospels, is an update. It is not a piece of historical research. It is a contemporary proclamation for the current community of Jesus believers. It addresses their concerns and questions, provides solace to them in their sorrows and dilemmas, offers hope to them in their doubts and confusions. We read the gospels differently when we realize that their intention was not to reconstruct the time when Jesus lived and taught but to tell the story of Jesus within the context of the believers' own fears, concerns, and hopes.

Why did Matthew write this gospel? Why did he not simply continue to use Mark as the community's source book, accompanied perhaps by his copy of Q? The shortest answer can be simply stated: the message needed to be expanded, restated, and updated for a new time and place. German scholars speak of a text's *Sitz im Leben.* In English, we call this a life-world, that is, a text's entire political, sociological, economic, and theological context. It's obvious that these life-worlds change. This means that telling a story from one life-world to another entails retelling the story. It is ironic but true that the only way to be faithful to a text is *not* to be faithful to it: not to literally repeat it in a context where the life-world is different.

Matthew's life-world in the 80s was dramatically different from Jesus's life-world in the late 20s. The Temple had been destroyed in the year 70 C.E. The Sadducees (the priestly leadership) had lost their primary function as a result of the cessation of animal sacrifices in the wake of the Temple's destruction. The Pharisees, a lay group of reform-minded Jews at the time of Jesus, were emerging in a new leadership role in the larger Jewish community, recognized as "the rabbis," that is, "the teachers." Matthew's community competed with these rabbis and their followers. They had radically different views on what faithfulness to God meant at this important juncture in Jewish history. The message of Jesus had to be proclaimed again in this new life-world; new gospel was needed.

Matthew's community, unlike Paul's churches, continued to be Torah observant, but the Torah had to be interpreted anew in light of the coming of the messianic age inaugurated by Jesus. Had not Jesus himself given his followers some principles for interpreting the commandments of the Torah? Had he not stressed the role of mercy and compassion, highlighting the Torah commandment (Leviticus 19:18) to love one's neighbor as oneself? Matthew proclaims a new way of God-centeredness; he sees his community mandated to communicate that message to Gentiles and Jews alike. He may, however, be convinced that few of his fellow Jews will accept this faith until the Messiah comes again as history's final judge.

Matthew as Propaganda

Is this gospel Jewish or anti-Jewish? The answer to the question is both. A great paradox runs through its twenty-eight chapters. This gospel is, at once, the most Jewish and the most anti-Jewish of the twenty-seven books in the Christian Testament. Countless features connect the text to the Jewish milieu of Jesus himself—including passages where Jesus seems to have no interest in the non-Jewish world bordering his own arena of experience. On the other hand, the fact that Jesus is called *rabbi* only twice (both times by Judas, his betrayer) leaves little room to doubt the hostility festering in this text toward those Jews who reject the faith it expresses.

How can one text contain such divergent perspectives? The short answer is that the gospel is a layered document, a palimpsest. Another image that may be helpful is to imagine the gospel having different strata of material, like an archaeological site with different layers of artifacts. The later strata of the gospel contain the more polemical passages. To put this in terms of what we discussed earlier, the anti-Jewish material stems more from the life-world of Matthew's community (the 80s) than from that of the historical Jesus (the 20s).

What this means—and this can be difficult for some readers to accept—is that Matthew's gospel, along with being many other things, is propaganda. The word carries a sinister tone for most of us today, but its root meaning is simply to continue something, to expand or extend it. Matthew's gospel, written in Greek, was meant to be propagated everywhere Greek was spoken; and that meant the length and breadth of the Roman Empire. The problem, of course, was that the movement's founder, Jesus of Nazareth, was arrested and executed as a political threat by a Roman prefect—hardly an attractive entrance to the hearts and minds of most Roman citizens.

Matthew handles this problem by downplaying the hostile role of the occupying Roman forces, especially in the events leading to Jesus's arrest and execution. Imagine yourself reading a story set in France during the time of the Nazi occupation in World War II. Further imagine that this story concerns a French peasant, a simple villager known for his kindness to others and for his homespun wisdom. Strangely enough, throughout this story, nothing negative is said or implied about the occupying forces. As a matter of fact, the French peasant is finally killed by the Germans only because crowds of French citizens clamor outside the Nazi headquarters demanding his death. Such a story seems difficult to imagine, yet it strongly resembles the story one finds in Matthew.

To facilitate the message's movement into the Roman Empire, criticism of Rome was suppressed. The tragic events leading to Jesus's arrest and death, therefore, had to have another cause. The only available group turned out to be Jesus's own people, his fellow Jews. Reading Matthew's gospel, we see that it is indeed Jesus's own people who willingly take responsibility for his death. When we add the later deification of Jesus by his followers, the Jewish crime escalates from killing a good man to killing God. This vilification of the Jewish people was less dangerous when Christianity was a persecuted sect within a pagan empire; but when the cross and crown were united in the fourth century, the propaganda soon became a sword of persecution.

This dimension of propaganda can no longer remain an academic secret. Christians are ethically bound not only to admit it but to teach it. How can that be done? Canonical texts cannot and should not be altered, but they must be interpreted and explained. And that means that whenever these texts are used, an effort must be made by the teacher or preacher to set the record straight. Honesty demands no less. Every form of replacement theology must be rejected so that Judaism can be acknowledged by Christians as a true and integral religion. Then Judaism can be rightly understood as a legitimate path of holiness, a sacred tradition, and an ongoing covenant.

Matthew as Mystagogue

A mystagogue is someone or something that leads us into mystery, initiating us or teaching us the way to its heart. Christians prepared for baptism in the early Roman church by a long period of study, climaxing with the baptism itself on the eve of Easter Sunday. The candidate (from *candidus,* the white robe worn in the ceremony) was immersed in the waters of the baptismal pool, anointed by deacons, and then brought to the bishop for the *traditio,* the "handing over." In this ceremony, a copy of the gospels was placed in the hands of the newly baptized Christians as a sign that they were now expected to live what they had studied.

In exploring Matthew's gospel, one notices that, along with its many divisions, it has a clear climactic moment when one of Jesus's disciples, Simon Peter, declares him to be God's anointed, the Messiah. This profession of faith forms the watershed of the gospel. Prior to this, we see Jesus largely as teacher, exorcist, healer, and holy man. After this, Jesus emerges as the man of sorrows, the one who must be handed over to suffer and die. This division marks a turning point in Christian initiation and, as well, represents a pivotal development in Jesus's career.

The structure of the gospel discloses an obvious path of instruction for the neophyte preparing to join Matthew's community. In the first half of the gospel, the candidate comes to appreciate Jesus as healer and helper; in the second half of the gospel, she must wrestle with the deeper issues of suffering and death. Love and loyalty must precede the commitment to risk and suffering. And the transition lies precisely in the gospel's center, where Peter acknowledges Jesus as Messiah. Once the candidate has accepted Jesus as God's anointed, then that person stands ready to take up the cross and to learn what it means to lose one's life in order to find it.

Matthew as a New Law

Religions and cultures in general have two kinds of norms operating together in the way they live their lives. One kind of norm is ethical and has to do with matters judged to be morally right or wrong. Another kind of norm is ceremonial or ritual and has to do with ways in which a given society defines itself. Catholic Christians, for example, realize the difference between murdering someone and eating meat on one of the Fridays of Lent. In our American society, there is a difference between the national debate about minimum wages and the discussions that take place about the proper treatment of the American flag. Many citizens fail to differentiate these two kinds of issues, but a minimum of reflection makes it clear that although both are important issues, they are in another sense "apples and oranges."

To put this in a biblical context, we must return to Leviticus. If we read chapters 11 to 20, we will probably find ourselves confused. We discover there a complex of laws involving everything from dietary restrictions (kashrut) to the handling of skin diseases to sexual matters to dealings with practitioners of magic arts. The first thing we have to realize is that what is confusing for us undoubtedly made sense within the context of the community preserving this tradition. It is much like traveling in a foreign county and being confused by the etiquette codes there while realizing, of course, that all of this makes as much sense to the natives as our own codes do to us.

What, then, brings all of this material together for the religious culture in which it has its original life-world? The phrase repeated again and again is a reminder to be holy because God is holy. What is the opposite of holy in this case? Clearly, not unethical or sinful or immoral, since the category of the ethical does not fit many of the behaviors that are either prescribed or proscribed—what does ethics have to do with whether or not a fish has scales? In the Hebrew Bible, a violation of holiness is called an abomination, something polluting the individual who commits it and possibly the community as well. And the integrity of community life as defined by these rules is understood by all members of that community.

Ethical commandments and holiness commandments are listed side by side in the Hebrew Bible. Even in the Ten Commandments, we can see a difference between Sabbath observance and murder. To know the difference between the two, we have to consider their consequences. If a Jew violates the Sabbath, both the individual and the community lose something of their identity. But if we fail to pay a hired worker right away, he and his family might starve or be thrown on the streets because of their inability to pay the rent. Ethical commands, in other words, entail injustice or lack of compassion toward other beings. When an ethical teaching is violated, someone is usually hurt, and this is why they are understood as sins.

Ethical discussions are thus transferable from one society to another in a way that holiness codes are not. In other words, we can discuss justice and compassion issues with people from another country more easily than we can discuss dietary practices. Hungry people in India refuse to eat their cows, just as hungry people in our inner cities generally stop short of eating stray cats. And yet neither behavior makes sense outside of the culture. But citizens of India and of the United States of America could both discuss the problems caused by abusing children, mistreating women, and underpaying workers.

Let us contrast an ethical issue then—like the example of paying a worker a just wage—with holiness issues. If an observant Jew eats the wrong kind of fish, it is "an abomination" (the normal biblical term employed), a violation of what constitutes Jews as a holy people and what, in some instances at least, distinguishes them from those who live outside their holiness covenant. But whether or not a fish has scales does not entail either injustice or lack of compassion toward other beings. Some may claim that eating the fish raises an ethical issue, but that is another matter. The criterion of having or not having scales on the fish is simply not an ethical issue that non-Jews can be expected to relate to in any way.

Lack of reflection on these differences leads to a great deal of confusion, prejudice, and pain in some areas of national debate today. For example, one form of male homogenital behavior (anal intercourse) is condemned in Leviticus 18:22, right in the middle of numerous regulations ranging from having sexual relations with a woman during her menstrual period to offering one's children in a fiery sacrifice to Moloch. Most of the people who quote this verse have no intent of abiding by all the other regulations surrounding it. And yet it is clearly a holiness regulation, not a moral one. Nor does the text speak to the issue of sexual orientation, but rather to a particular form of behavior that was considered inappropriate in that culture.

Forbidding men to perform certain homogenital acts with other men parallels not mixing meat and dairy products or not sewing two diverse kinds of material in the same garment. These things are an abomination because they violate distinctions seen as defining characteristics of a particular society, giving it its identity, its wholeness, and thus its holiness. We have to understand, however, that once we no longer affirm that kind of society in its entirety, it is in no way automatic that a particular piece of holiness legislation should be transferred to another society, religion, or culture. Once we drop the ethical dimension, then we face a new kind of question in asking ourselves whether a different sexual orientation (something the Bible never discusses) should be an abomination in our society and, if so, on what grounds.

This same section of Leviticus has a thorough discussion of fluids emanating from our bodies. It does not take too much study of the text to realize that menstruating women, men experiencing nocturnal seminal emissions, and people with running sores are all guilty of abominations. This does not make them morally "bad" or unethical in any way. Abominations fall under a different category. I often wish that Catholic moralists had realized this when I was in high school. It struck terror in our hormonally driven adolescent hearts when priests gave sermons in which they told us that acts of masturbation were the nails that fastened Jesus to the cross. One thinks of all those centuries of Catholic guilt that could have been avoided by the simple realization that masturbation has nothing to do with ethics.

In saying that these holiness issues are not ethical, are we implying that they are automatically of less importance? Not necessarily. Within the ancient revelational context (still affirmed by observant Jews today), both ethical commands and holiness commands come from the same God. The radical character of Paul's break with his Jewish tradition lay precisely in his abandonment of these codes for his Gentile converts while requiring them to adhere to the ethical commands. This is not to say that Paul did not establish holiness codes for his churches—and sometimes he clearly imported practices from his own Jewish tradition—but the point is that he did not see the holiness codes as mandatory for non-Jewish Christians.

What about Matthew? He sees the Jesus way as preserving both moral and holiness codes. He knows that Jesus's emphasis is on inwardness or intentionality, but he knows too that Jesus lived as an observant Jew. We will see in the text certain acts of Jesus that challenge certain interpretations of the holiness codes, but never do we see Jesus deny or abrogate them. So Matthew's gospel, like the community that produced it, stands in sharp contrast to the Pauline writings, where the holiness codes have been superseded—at least for Gentile converts.

The Translation

Translation is an inevitable path to frustration, and the best advice is the recommendation that people learn the original language—in this case, Greek—or ask them to read diverse translations, recognizing that each of them attempts to pick up some nuance of the original. This latter advice I find more realistic for most of my readers. I do not intend my translation to replace any of the excellent translations already available. It is my hope, however, that it can highlight certain features of the text not captured in other versions.

Matthew's Greek is frustratingly simple. Any translator grows weary of the constantly recurring "and then," wishing that the gospel's author had learned more about building transitions. The challenge to the translator is not rendering the Greek in literal English but attempting to produce a translation in language that is recognizable to speakers of American English in the twenty-first century. At the same time, the translator must avoid some of the passing fads of language, dooming a translation to irrelevance within a few years.

Martin Luther, the great translator of both the Hebrew Bible and the Christian Testament into German, once remarked that he would walk by the shops of the baker and the blacksmith, listen to how people conversed there, and then return to his study to render the Hebrew or Greek text before him in the idioms he had just heard on the street. Certainly the genius of his masterful translation lies partly in the way it speaks so directly to the German-language reader.

All translation is interpretation, and all interpretation is in some sense a betrayal of the original text. As the Italian proverb states it, every *traduttore* is a *traditore:* every translator is a traitor. The question is always one of limits; in other words, how far does one want to go in interpreting?

Take as an example Matthew 5:15, the familiar text reminding us that one does not light a lamp to put it under a bushel. One can be inventive in finding the right word to translate *modios*—a bowl, a bushel, or a bucket. People at the time used a *modios* to cover and thereby extinguish a small oil lamp. So perhaps the best rendering of this text is simply "No one lights a lamp and then immediately extinguishes it."

In addition to producing readable American English, another conscious goal of my translation is to clarify the connection to Jewish names and customs often obscured by current translations. This is why Jesus becomes Jeshu in my translation. His full name was Jehoshua ben Josef: Joshua the son of Joseph. But Jehoshua was commonly shortened to Jeshua or Jeshu. When the gospels were written in Greek, there was a problem. Greek has no *sh* sound. So *Jesu* was the closest approximation to *Jeshu*. Furthermore, it was not common in Greek to end a name in a vowel, and the word *Jesus* was arrived at. In similar fashion, *baptism* becomes *immersion,* thereby allowing the link to the parallel use of immersion in both Judaism and Christianity to be evident. Too often Jesus falls between two chairs, his Judaism recognized neither by Jews nor by Christians.

The Hidden
Gospel of Matthew

1 The first words of Matthew's gospel are *biblos geneseos,* and they are usually translated "an account of the genealogy." The Greek word *geneseos,* however, is the possessive form of the word *genesis,* which we all know as the Greek title of the first book of the Bible. There are various indications that the author of this gospel is writing this book as a new Torah, and so it may not be a mere coincidence that he begins the gospel with this word, the first word of the Hebrew Bible.

⚭ This gospel, like the other twenty-six books of the Christian Testament, is written in Greek, since that was the language commonly spoken in the Roman Empire during the first century of the Common Era (C.E., which is equivalent to A.D.).

2 He is proclaimed in this text as the Messiah, one who is anointed with oil, chosen by God for a role of kingly leadership. The Greek translation of this word is *Christos,* and this gives us the full title in Greek: *Jesus ho Christos,* or Jesus the Messiah, or Jesus the Christ. And so it is that most of the world knows this man today as Jesus Christ. *Christ,* however, is not a second name but a title. In this translation, he will be known as Jeshu the Messiah.

⚭ What did it mean to proclaim Jeshu as Messiah? Initially it was the kings, and later the priests, who were anointed with oil. As political sovereignty was withheld from the Jewish people through successive domination by Babylonians, Persians, Hellenists, and Romans, the whole idea of the anointed king became more of a hope for the future than a fact for the present; and so it is that this increasingly deferred hope is invested with progressively higher expectations. Wrestling the political rule from foreigners, establishing justice and true peace, cleansing the land of idolatry, and announcing the truth of Torah to the whole world—all of this falls to the expected Messiah.

3 Seeking more gender-inclusive language, I will often translate *son* as *child.* The author wants us to know through this genealogy that

(continued on page 4)

1 □ Complicated and Paradoxical Beginnings (Matthew 1:1–4:25)

The genesis[1] of Jeshu the Messiah,[2] the child of David and of Abraham.[3]

(continued on page 5)

3

Jeshu is the descendant both of David and of Abraham. In other words, he is a true Jew (thus a descendant of Abraham) and an anointed king (thus a descendant of David). Since the author is a student of the Hebrew Bible, he naturally sees Jeshu in the light of biblical figures.

4 Five women are mentioned in the genealogy: Tamar, Rahab, Ruth, Bathsheba (she is not mentioned by name but as "the wife of Uriah") and Miriam, Jeshu's mother. Now if any women were to be mentioned, one might expect Sarah, Rebecca, and Rachel, the great matriarchs of the Jewish people. Not only are these three exemplary women not mentioned, but it must be admitted that those chosen to be included seem less than apt candidates for Judaism's social register. Tamar poses as a prostitute and Rahab is one; Ruth and Bathsheba are foreigners. Does this cast some aspersions on Miriam, too? Does it suggest some taint on Jeshu's birth? Was there something unusual about the birth of Jeshu?

5 Something seems odd about a genealogy that painstakingly traces the whole Jewish history down to Josef and then suddenly drops him, denoting simply that he is the husband of Miriam and that it was of her, and not presumably of Josef, that Jeshu was born. What is happening here? The most obvious explanation is that the original genealogy ended with Jeshu as the child of Josef, but the later development of a virgin-birth story called for an alternative ending. This is our first clear example of the palimpsest character of this text: an earlier message has been modified because of a later perspective.

6 Why this explicit reference to three groups of fourteen? The third group, by the way, does not even come out to fourteen unless you count Jehoiachin a second time (since he was the fourteenth in group two as well). We know that Hebrew letters were also used as numbers, and thus each word in Hebrew is also a numerical sum. The word *David* is composed of three Hebrew letters whose sum is fourteen. So by a kind of scribal pun, we can infer that this is the genealogy of someone who is three times fourteen and therefore three times David.

(continued on page 6)

Abraham was the father of Isaac, Isaac of Jacob, and Jacob of Judah and his brothers. It was by Tamar[4] that Judah fathered Perez and Zerah; Hezron was Perez' son, and Hezron's son was Ram. Ram was the father of Amminadab, Amminadab of Nahshon, and Nahshon of Salmon. Salmon fathered Boaz by Rahab, and Boaz' son by Ruth was Obed. Obed was the father of Jesse, whose son was King David.

It was by the wife of Uriah that David fathered Solomon, and Solomon's son was Rehoboam, the father of Abijah, whose son was Asa. Asa was the father of Jehoshaphat, Jehoshaphat of Joram, and Joram of Uzziah. Uzziah was the father of Jotham, Jotham of Ahaz, and Ahaz of Hezekiah. Hezekiah fathered Manasseh, whose son was Amon, the father of Josiah. Josiah was the father of Jehoiachin and his brothers, at the time of the Babylonian Exile.

After that exile, Jehoiachin fathered Shealtiel, whose son was Zerubbabel. Zerubbabel was the father of Abiud, Abiud of Eliakim, Eliakim of Azor, Azor of Zadok, Zadok of Achim, and Achim of Eliud. Eliud fathered Eleazar, whose son was Matthan, whose son was Jacob. Jacob fathered Josef, Miriam's husband, and of her was born Jeshu, who is called the Messiah.[5]

So all together there are fourteen generations from Abraham to David, fourteen from David to the Babylonian Exile, and fourteen from the Babylonian Exile to the Messiah.[6]

(continued on page 7)

Now since David was God's anointed king, or messiah, and the model for all future messiahs, who could be three times David but the promised and long-awaited Messiah himself?

⚠ Are all the circumstances of Jeshu's life up to the time of his immersion in the waters of the Jordan simply unknown? And, in that case, is Matthew developing a midrash featuring Jeshu as the fulfillment of certain specific texts from the Hebrew Bible? Does Matthew's use of a prophetic text about a virgin birth paint him into a corner, where he has to explain the consequences of dropping the human father from the birth story? An affirmative answer to these three questions leads to a satisfying explanation of Matthew's story—namely, that it is pure midrash, offering us no historical information about the actual circumstances of Jeshu's birth.

On the other hand, were there unusual circumstances surrounding the birth of Jeshu about which there are some historical remembrances? In that case, would not Matthew have to prepare us for the consequences of jumping to the kind of conclusions anyone might expect from that kind of story? And is that what the genealogy and this birth story are intended to accomplish? An affirmative answer to these three questions leads to the conclusion that Matthew in this case deals with some problematic but historical realities. This is one of many instances where peeling off a layer of text or paint seems particularly challenging.

Whatever approach one takes, these opening verses are fraught with challenges for the reader. Matthew clearly wants to introduce Jeshu as a true Jew, a child of Abraham. At the same time, Jeshu fulfills the deepest longings attached to the title of Messiah and thus is the true child of David as well. Most deeply, however, Jeshu is God's child. From the perspective of Matthew's faith, there is something clearly miraculous about this birth. From the human perspective, however, an aura of suspicion and even of scandal seems to surround this story. Controversy characterizes this gospel from its first chapter to its last.

This was how the birth of Jeshu the Messiah took place. When his mother Miriam had been engaged to Josef, but before they were living together, she became pregnant by a holy spirit. Her husband Josef, being a God-centered person and not wanting to disgrace her, resolved to break off the engagement with as little publicity as possible. But while he was contemplating this, an angel of the Lord appeared to him in a dream and said, "Josef, son of David, don't be afraid to take Miriam as your wife, for the child she carries is from a holy spirit. A son will be born to her, and you will name him Jeshu, because he will save his people from their sins."

(continued on page 9)

7 The scandal in Matthew's narrative moves to center stage as we realize that the people with whom Miriam and Josef lived knew how to count. Since they had received no angelic visitations, they certainly had every reason to conclude that Jeshu was born too soon to have been conceived after the marriage of his parents. What explanation does Matthew offer for Jeshu's conception before his parents' marriage? Josef, precisely because he is God-centered, is understandably upset with this inexplicable pregnancy. He (like his namesake in Genesis) draws on his ability to interpret dreams to come to peace with a pregnancy not of his own doing. The teaching of a virgin birth is introduced to explain what has happened, and Matthew supports this with a verse from scripture, which, in the Greek translation then current in his Jewish world, uses the word *parthenos,* usually translated "virgin," (whereas the original Hebrew *almah* means nothing more than "young girl"). The answer to the scandal, then, is that Mary, while still a virgin, conceived Jeshu by a holy spirit, presumably without any act of sexual intercourse. Thus we have added the story of a virgin birth—something the earlier Christian Testament writers, like Mark and Paul, do not mention.

⚖ I find midrash here rather than history, sermonic material rather than fact. Midrash, of course, has its own kind of truth, and in no way is it to be dismissed as mere fable or fiction. Midrash tells the story that calls to us between the lines and words of the received text; it fills the gaps in the original story. And since all of Jeshu's life up to the age of thirty is gap, early Christian writers had a field day in filling such an inviting space. Another thirty gospels are not found in the Christian Testament, and some of these noncanonical gospels are filled with fantastic infancy stories, far excelling anything found in Matthew or Luke.

Now all of this had come about to fulfill what God spoke through his prophet: "Look, a young woman will become pregnant and bear a son, who will be called Immanuel." This name means "God is with us." So when Josef woke up, he did what the angel told him and took Miriam as his wife. And yet, they didn't have any sexual relations up to the time that she gave birth to the child to whom Josef gave the name Jeshu.[7]

(continued on page 11)

8 Matthew has things to tell us, and he employs midrash as a popular literary genre of his time. He wants us to know that Jeshu is the Messiah, and since we have already seen that the Messiah is David "writ large," or "three times David's fourteen," we must also realize that this child must be born in Bethlehem, since that is David's city. After all, was it not from Bethlehem's fields that David, Jesse's youngest son, was called by the prophet Samuel and anointed as king?

9 Matthew lives in a community of Christians where most are born Jews, though a few are undoubtedly non-Jews or Gentiles who—much like those first seers—"saw the light." The seers are the ancestors of all Gentile believers. They bring their gifts to the child in whom they recognize God's presence. Not having a sociological relationship to the traditions that make sense out of messiahs, their discernment seems all the more laudable. They are the first Gentiles we meet as actual characters in the gospel. As in this story, Gentiles make only cameo appearances in Matthew's narrative, since the main action is always carried by Jews—another indication of the predominantly Jewish ethnicity of Matthew's community.

10 This midrash presents a parody of the Exodus story, where we find Jewish slaves fleeing from an Egyptian king to the land that will become Israel. In that story an Egyptian king seeks to kill a Jewish baby, Moses. In Matthew's story, the baby who embodies all of Israel's—and indeed all of the world's—hopes flees from an evil Jewish king who has ordered his death. He comes to find refuge in the very land from which his ancestors fled. We see here the first indication of the anti-Jewish story that Matthew is adding to the original story of Jeshu the Jew. The resistance of some of the Jewish leadership to Jeshu's message has been symbolically placed at the very beginning of Jeshu's story through this fanciful but instructive midrash.

11 Josef was wise to fear going to Judea, where Archelaus was in charge. Archelaus was one of the three Herodian princes who shared their father's kingdom after the death of Herod the Great in 4 B.C.E. Archelaus ruled the southern half of his father's former kingdom (including Judea, with its capital city of Jerusalem), and his brother Herod Antipas governed the Galilee and Perea, and his other brother, Philip, ruled over territories east of the Jordan River. The word was certainly out that Archelaus was more despicable than his brother Herod Antipas. He was known to be an apple that had not fallen far from the tree; in other words, he was almost as cruel and vicious as his father. By 6 C.E. everyone was fed up with him, including the Romans, and the emperor sent Archelaus into exile in Gaul. The whole southern territory thus came under direct Roman rule in the form of the Roman prefect of Syria.

12 Jochanan is familiar to most readers of the Christian Testament as John. Here again, the use of the Hebrew name links the many characters in the Christian Testament who bear that name with near-contemporary Jewish figures such as the great Pharisee Jochanan ben Zakkai. Calling this Jochanan "the Baptist" can only lead to confusion. Southern Baptists constitute the second-largest Christian denomination in the United States today, but this Jochanan was not of their number, nor was Jochanan performing the sacrament of Christian baptism. Thus, in my translation he becomes Jochanan the Immerser. The word *baptisma* in Greek translates the Hebrew word *tvila*, both of which mean "immersion."

⚜ This entire immersion story comes from Q, the source shared by Luke and Matthew but not used by Mark. In Luke, Jochanan speaks to "the crowds," offering specific advice to tax-collectors and to soldiers. Matthew deletes these two groups as well as the job-specific advice, keeping only the angry words of judgment redirected now from "the crowds" to the Pharisees and Sadducees (who are completely absent in Luke's version of this story). This polemic against the Jewish leadership fits Matthew's life-world in the 80s far better than it does Jochanan's in the 20s.

In the days of King Herod, Jeshu was born in Bethlehem[8] of Ju
Seers[9] from the east came to Jerusalem, asking, "Where is the one t
to be king of the Jews? We've seen his rising star and are here to ho
him." When King Herod heard this, he was upset, as was all
Jerusalem. Calling together all the chief priests and Torah schola
Herod asked them where the Messiah was to be born. "In Bethlehem
Judea," they told him. "For this is what the prophet wrote: 'And yc
Bethlehem, in the land of Judah, are far from the least among Juda
leading cities, for from you will come a leader who will shepherd n
people Israel.'"

At this point Herod secretly brought in the seers and asked thei
when this star first appeared. Then he sent them to Bethlehem with th
request "Go and search carefully for the child and let me know whei
you have found him, so that I too might come and honor him." Wher
the seers heard what the king had to say, they set out, and the same
star they had seen before led them to the place where the child was.

They were incredibly happy when they saw the star again, and on
entering the house and seeing the child with Miriam, his mother, they
prostrated themselves and honored him. They opened their treasures
and offered him gifts of gold, incense, and myrrh. Afterward, since they
had been warned in a dream not to go back to Herod, they took a different road home to their own country.

As soon as they had gone, an angel of the Lord appeared to Josef
in a dream and said, "Get up! Take the child and his mother, and flee to
Egypt. Stay there until I give you further word. Herod wants to kill the
child and will be looking for him." Josef got up, took the child and his
mother while it was still night, and left for Egypt. He stayed there until
Herod's death. This was to fulfill what the Lord said through the
prophet: "I have called my child out of Egypt."[10]

(continued on page 1)

When Herod realized that he had been tricked by the seers, he was furious. He ordered the death of every boy under two years old in Bethlehem and all its surrounding neighborhoods, calculating the time according to what he had learned from the seers. It was then that the words of the prophet Jeremiah were fulfilled: "A voice was heard in Ramah, the sound of bitter weeping. Rachel crying for her children and refusing to be comforted, because they are no more."

As soon as Herod was dead, an angel of the Lord appeared in a dream to Josef in Egypt, saying: "Get up! Take the child and his mother and return to the land of Israel, for those who sought the life of the child are dead." So Josef got up, took the child and his mother, and went back to the land of Israel. When Josef heard that Archelaus[11] was ruling in Judea in place of his father, Herod, he was afraid to go there. So when he received a warning in a dream, he went to the Galilee, going to a town called Nazareth, in fulfillment of what was said by the prophets: "He shall be called a Nazorean."

Some time later, Jochanan the Immerser went into the Judean desert, telling people, "Turn your lives around; the reign of God is approaching."[12]

(continued on page 15)

13 In the life-world of Jeshu, Jewish leadership was represented by the Pharisees and Sadducees, with the Essenes playing a significant role as well. As traditional enemies, the Pharisees and Sadducees would not have been likely to stroll down to the river together. This fanciful element is added by Matthew to Mark's account. At the time Matthew's gospel was written, the Temple had been destroyed and the power of both Sadducees and Essenes had been virtually eliminated. The Pharisees, however, had survived to become the rabbis of the emerging form of Judaism, representing the greatest challenge to Matthew's interpretation of their shared Jewish history. Thus, the Pharisees are criticized by Matthew far more than any other group.

14 This passionate prophet stands midstream in the apocalyptic period of Jewish writings, spanning approximately three hundred years from 150 B.C.E. to 150 C.E. An apocalypse unveils or uncovers (the literal meaning of the Greek) a vision of the future in which the divine judgment is poised to enter human history dramatically. Immediate alignment with the divine order is required of us. We must decide where our loyalty lies, and act decisively. No reliance on ancestry (as children of Abraham) or rank (as a hereditary priest or levite) carries any validity. We must either demonstrate the fruits of a God-centered life or be cut down by an ax poised to fall, a fork ready to sweep clean the threshing floor.

15 Embarrassment is one of the criteria by which biblical scholars determine the authenticity of a tradition. In other words, no writer invents a story that would prove an embarrassment to the community for which he is writing. Therefore, any story that would be embarrassing to the community telling it more likely comes from an earlier tradition. The immersion by Jochanan signifies turning from sin to a path of God-centered living. It is clearly an embarrassment for the early Christians that the sinless Jeshu came to Jochanan for a ritual immersion. Therefore, this strange logic contends that Jeshu was almost certainly immersed by him in the waters of the Jordan. This part of the story, in terms of our palimpsest metaphor, is on the original parchment.

(continued on page 16)

It was of this Jochanan that the prophet Isaiah spoke when he said, "The voice of one crying in the desert: prepare the way of the Lord, make his paths straight." Jochanan's clothes were made of camel hair, and he wore an animal-hide belt around his waist. His diet consisted of locusts and wild honey. Many people went out to see him—people from Jerusalem, from the whole province of Judea, and from the area around the Jordan River. They publicly admitted their sins and were immersed by him in the river. But when Jochanan saw many of the Pharisees and Sadducees[13] coming to be immersed, he said to them, "You brood of vipers! Who warned you to flee from the anger of God that's coming? Produce the fruit that comes from a real turning around of your life. Don't think that it's enough to say that Abraham is your father, for God can make children for Abraham from these desert rocks. Already the ax has been laid to the root of the trees, and every tree failing to produce good fruit will be cut down and thrown into the fire. I immerse you in water for the turning around of your lives, but the one coming after me will immerse you in the fire of a holy spirit. He is so much greater than me that I am not good enough even to carry his sandals. His winnowing fork is in his hand, ready to clear his threshing floor; he will gather the wheat into his barn and burn the chaff with a fire that never goes out."[14]

Sometime later, Jeshu came from the Galilee and stood before Jochanan at the Jordan to be immersed by him. Jochanan tried to stop him, saying, "I ought to be immersed by you, and yet you come to me!"[15] But Jeshu answered him, "Let things alone for now; this way we'll be doing all that God requires."

(continued on page 17)

Matthew's embarrassment of the received text leads him to add the element of Jochanan's hesitancy, along with Jeshu's contrived response that they should keep up appearances. This secondary narrative layer casts God in an awkward light for requiring such a charade. If we accept the immersion at face value, but dismantle Matthew's careful scaffolding to cover the alleged scandal, the unembellished story suggests that Jeshu, like any other Jew of his time, went to the Jordan that day as a sign of turning completely to God and that he experienced there a profound and life-changing encounter with the divine reality.

16 The immersion is accompanied by what is known in the Jewish tradition as a *bat kol:* a voice from heaven. While Luke follows Mark by putting the voice in the second person, Matthew's decision to alter the Marcan version into the third person ("This is ..." rather than "You are ...") seems to imply that it is not so much Jeshu who is learning anything new from this message, but rather the bystanders and, ultimately, the readers of the gospel.

The message itself combines two scriptural traditions: Psalm 2, wherein the anointed king is told, "You are my Child," and Isaiah 42:1, wherein God's suffering servant is called "My chosen one, in whom I take delight." Thus, the idea of messiah from one text is added to the idea of God's suffering servant in another. The combination gives us something new: a suffering messiah.

More of Matthew's portrait of Jeshu is visible now. He is three times David: David's true descendant and Abraham's as well. He is also Miriam's child by a miraculous birth. Most important, however, he is God's Child, revealed as God's Messiah: one called to suffer in service to God, to his own people, and to all of humanity. It is on this Jeshu that the Divine Spirit settles with the gentleness of a dove.

So Jochanan went along with this, and as soon as Jeshu had been immersed, he came up out of the water. Then heaven opened up for Jeshu, and he saw a spirit of God coming down like a dove and resting on him. And a voice from heaven said: "This is my child, the child I love, the child in whom I take great delight."**16**

(continued on page 19)

17 The story of three temptations exists in both Matthew and Luke with little difference. We presume this minidrama comes from their shared source, Q, since Mark simply reports the event without any narrative of the temptations themselves. Jeshu may well have wanted some time alone after the powerful theophany accompanying his immersion experience. Anything beyond that seems midrashic, since no one was there to take notes. Jeshu's responses are quotations from Deuteronomy, possibly reflecting Matthew's intention to present Jeshu as the obedient Israel standing in sharp contrast to the disobedient Israel addressed by Moses in Deuteronomy.

Jeshu, God's true servant, demonstrates his obedience to God's word in this narrative of temptation. But it is important to notice that he is vulnerable as well. Our word *vulnerable* comes from the Latin word *vulnus,* meaning "wound." A vulnerable person is one who can be wounded—a condition consonant with Jeshu's vocation to be God's suffering Messiah, God's wounded healer. Consequently, Jeshu is unwilling to ask for special divine intervention, either for his own bodily needs (his hunger) or in a situation where bodily harm threatens (as in throwing himself down from a building).

The great spiritual traditions all seem to note our characteristic human frailty, rendering us so vulnerable to life's tests. The Hindus see us as ignorant, while the Buddhists claim that we are sleepy. The Muslims call us to pray five times a day because we are prone to forget that only God is God. Jews recognize an evil inclination, leading us to miss the mark (the root meaning of *sin* in Hebrew and Greek); and in Christianity this theme finds classic expression in the teaching of original sin. The final though unflattering truth about us seems to be that we are not a highly enlightened species when it comes to handling life's many tests. Like the Buddha when he is similarly tested, Jeshu handles life's tests with extraordinary skill and courage.

Then Jeshu was led by the Spirit into the desert, to be tempted by the Devil. After fasting there for forty days and nights he was hungry, and it was then that the tempter approached him and said, "If you are God's child, ask these stones to turn into loaves of bread." Jeshu answered, "Scripture says that we cannot live on bread alone but need every word that God speaks." Then the Devil took Jeshu to the holy city and placed him on an upper ledge of the Temple and said to him, "If you are God's child, throw yourself down, for scripture says that God's angels have been entrusted with your care and that their hands will catch you, so that not even your foot will strike a stone." Jeshu answered, "Scripture also says that you should not try to make the Lord your God prove that he cares for you." Once more the Devil took Jeshu, this time to a very high mountain, where he showed him an array of the world's powerful nations, and he said to him, "All this I'll give you, if you kneel down and worship me." Then Jeshu said to him, "Get away from me, Satan! Scripture tells us to worship the Lord our God and serve no one but God." At this point the Devil left Jeshu, while angels came and ministered to him.[17]

(continued on page 21)

18 A critical juncture is indicated in this passage, since Jeshu's spiritual mentor and teacher has now been arrested by Herod Antipas. The circumstances of that arrest are not important at this point, though Matthew will return to them later. Let us recap the primary historical facts in our narrative to this point. (1) Jeshu's public life emerged in the context of the ministry of Jochanan. (2) A powerful and initiatory theophany accompanied his immersion in the waters of the Jordan. (3) Jeshu retreated to the desert to wrestle with the implications of this newly perceived or recently confirmed relationship to the Divine. Now a fourth element is added as we see that Jochanan's arrest and subsequent removal from the scene have a powerful impact on Jeshu.

19 Reacting to this tragic turn of events, Jeshu leaves the south of Israel, site of the wilderness of his temptation, as well as the locus of Jochanan's ministry at the Jordan, and returns to his home territory in the north. Going home seems a natural enough move for someone who is distressed and disconcerted. And yet, in going home, Jeshu is moving from territory under direct control of the Roman procurator to an area ruled by the same Herod Antipas who arrested Jochanan. Interestingly, however, he does not return to his own hometown of Nazareth. He might well have feared for himself or his family if he went to his hometown. By going to a city near the north end of the Sea of Galilee, Jeshu was much closer to the territory ruled by Herod Antipas's brother, Philip, and could easily escape into that territory if he heard that soldiers were on the way to arrest him.

20 It is possible that Jeshu is returning to the Galilee after a long absence, perhaps after several years spent with the Essenes, in the company of Jochanan, or in a desert hermitage of his own. Does he see his homeland with new eyes when he returns? The bustling city of Sepphoris with its hellenized culture, including both gymnasium and amphitheater, lies just a few miles from Jeshu's hometown of Nazareth. Herod's building projects must have impressed Jeshu's fellow Galileans with the power and magnificence of Caesar's reign. Does the growth of this commercial expansion of Caesar's reign in his homeland lead Jeshu

(continued on page 22)

After this, hearing of Jochanan's arrest,[18] Jeshu withdrew into the Galilee.[19] He did not stay in Nazareth but went to live in Kapharnahum, a town by the Lake of Galilee, in the tribal lands of Zebulun and Naphtali. This was done to fulfill what the prophet Isaiah had said: "Land of Zebulun, land of Naphtali, the lake road, across the Jordan, Galilee, land of the Gentiles. The people who dwell in darkness have seen a great light; for those who sat in the shadowland of death, light has dawned." From that time on, Jeshu began to proclaim the message, "Turn your lives around; the reign of God[20] is approaching."

(continued on page 23)

to focus increasingly on the contrasting reign of God? If so, what precisely is the meaning of the reign that Jeshu now proclaims?

Our text shows Jeshu apparently proclaiming the identical message
that Jochanan proclaimed before him. But was this indeed the case? I
am inclined to the view that Jeshu's preaching had some orientation to
a future reign of God but was primarily directed to a present reality. These
two perspectives, in the last analysis, are complementary, not contradic-
tory. No present moment, after all, exists for us as human beings except
within a horizon of future—a future entailing some form of death and
confrontation with eternity. This reign of which Jeshu speaks, then, can
have implications for both present and future realities.

21 A transition has taken place here, but it is implied more than described.
Jeshu has apparently realized that he is now more than a disciple of
Jochanan. Beginning, therefore, to exercise a new kind of leadership, he
chooses his own disciples, men who will serve as an outreach of his own
ministry. Precisely what that ministry entails and how it differs from the
ministry of his mentor is something that remains to be seen.

While he was walking near the Lake of Galilee,[21] Jeshu saw two brothers, Shimon, called "Rock," and his brother Andri. Being fishermen, they were throwing their net into the lake.

(continued on page 25)

22 The image of fishing for people might strike us as a bit perverse. After all, a caught fish loses both freedom and life in providing food for the fisherman. But even if the image is less than perfect, the idea seems clear enough. The energies of these four men had been directed to fish; Jeshu now calls them to share a ministry in which people, not fish, will provide the focus of their labors. More important, pulling fish from water entails a transition from one element to another—that is, forces moving from the unconscious to consciousness. This movement describes an immersion in reverse, thus suggesting a birthing. Something new appears to be coming into being around this man from the Galilee.

⚬ In this passage we see Jeshu for the first time as the initiator of activity. How did his fellow Jews see him? Many of us are so used to the language of Christian theology that we almost imagine people turning from their fishing or farming to notice the Son of God or the Second Person of the Blessed Trinity. Such was hardly the case. But whom did they see? How would Jeshu have been understood in his own lifeworld? When we ride the commuter train in the morning, we can usually tell the difference between bankers and shoe salespersons, between brokers and department store personnel. When people like Shimon, Andri, Jacob, and Jochanan looked up from their fishing nets, they saw a Jewish peasant, perhaps even a dispossessed peasant, one of the destitute homeless who filled this land darkened by the clouds of Roman occupation and tyranny, the shadow side of the magnificent buildings, aqueducts, and roads. Perhaps because of Jeshu's association with Jochanan, people also saw a holy man, what Judaism calls a hasid. There were other hasids (in Hebrew, *hasidim*) in the Galilee. They were men of prayer, intimate with God, rejecting material comforts, often engaged in healing, and usually attracting a group of disciples.

Jeshu said to them, "Follow me, and I'll teach you to fish for people."[22] They immediately dropped their fishing gear and followed him. Then Jeshu went farther on and saw two other brothers, Jacob and his brother Jochanan. They were Zebedee's sons and were in the boat with their father, mending their nets. Jeshu called them, and immediately leaving both boat and father behind, they followed him.

(continued on page 27)

23 This is not the last time that we will see the anachronistic phrase "their synagogues." Surely these were "his" synagogues, too. In this instance, the usage seems to be picked up from Mark's gospel. Nevertheless, as we read further in Matthew, we will feel this sense of separation from rabbinic Judaism ever more intensely. The distance undoubtedly belongs more to the life-world of Matthew's community than to the life-world of Jeshu. By the late first century, Matthew's community of Christians realizes that the interpretation of Judaism they represent is not making much headway among most of their fellow Jews. They see the organization of many of the synagogues under rabbinic leadership after the year 70 c.e. both as a rejection of their own understanding and as an embodiment of a powerful rival. This distancing will become more dangerous and even disastrous when this movement departs from the world of Judaism, becoming an almost totally Gentile enterprise in the following centuries.

& Few things seem more certain about Jeshu than his role as healer. Our contemporary world is so fragmented that many of us go to psychiatrists with our psychological problems, to a variety of doctors with our various physical symptoms, and to a clergyperson with our spiritual concerns. Such dichotomies did not exist in Jeshu's life-world. This coincidence of physical healing and forgiveness of sins was assumed by the rabbis well into the third century.

There is no doubt that the presence of Jeshu brought healing to human beings in every aspect of their being. After all, *salvus,* the Latin root of our word *salvation,* means "well," "sound," and "safe," as well as "saved." The sanitized and separated sense of "salvation" that one finds in later Christian doctrine (i.e., saving one's soul for heaven) was quite foreign to Jeshu's life-world. Just as his ministry entailed total presence to those he met, so did it offer holistic healing to those touched by his compassionate concern.

Jeshu traveled all around the Galilee, teaching in their synagogues,[23] announcing the good news of God's reign, and healing every
kind of sickness and infirmity found among the people there. His repu-
tation spread through the whole province of Syria, and people brought
to him all those who were sick and suffering from all kinds of diseases
and pains—people possessed by demons, epileptics, paralytics—and
Jeshu healed them. Large crowds followed him, from the Galilee and the
Decapolis, from Jerusalem and the whole area of Judea, and from the
territories on the other side of the Jordan.

1 These teachings were never the content of one "sermon" delivered by Jeshu, nor were they given "on a mount" (in Luke's version, the teachings are delivered on a plain). Matthew has five such collections of material in his text, reflecting the five books of Torah in the Jewish tradition. Jeshu "went up on a mount" for this first sermon because Moses ascended a mountain to receive the first Torah, a teaching that for Matthew has been fulfilled in the messianic Torah of Jeshu.

2 This first "sermon" begins with a series of blessings. There are other such lists of blessings both in the Hebrew Bible and in the Dead Sea Scrolls. What seems unusual, however, in Jeshu's use of this convention is the shocking reversal of normal measures of success (or blessing, in the more literal translation). Most people know this collection of blessings as the Beatitudes. The word comes from the Latin *beatitudo*, meaning "blessedness" or "happiness." "Blessed" seems too far from ordinary speech, and "happy" does not seem serious enough for the context. What Americans take most seriously is success, and so my final translation choice is "successful."

3 The first blessing is key, since it points to the receptivity required to receive any teaching. This poverty is more than an empty wallet. It's an openness to all that God has to offer. Without spiritual receptivity, no teaching can find a place in our hearts. The second beatitude, like all those that follow the first, is in the future tense, while the first is in the present tense. In one sense, the first beatitude excels all the others and includes all the others. From one side it is emptiness; from the other side it is the reign of God. To the extent to which we are emptiness— without ego, without dogma, without the restrictions of the habitual— we are the spaciousness, the vastness, the pure sky, which is God and God's reign. There's no future tense here; this is all present, all right now. To understand this first beatitude is to understand the other six; indeed, it is to understand all of Jeshu's teachings.

☖ A Buddhist story aptly illustrates the centrality of this thematic receptivity. A king hears that a famous Buddhist teacher is in his territory.

(continued on page 30)

2 □ The World's Greatest Sermon
(Matthew 5:1-7:29)

Seeing what a crowd there was, Jeshu went up on the mount[1] and sat down, and his disciples gathered around him. He then began to teach them, saying: "You're successful[2] if you're spiritually receptive; you have room for God's reign.[3]

(continued on page 31)

Desiring the prestige of entertaining such a person, the king invites him to the palace for tea. The teacher accepts, though knowing full well the character of his host and the reason for the invitation. When the teacher arrives at court, the king asks him to pour tea for the two of them. The teacher complies and begins to pour tea into the king's cup, but he keeps pouring, even when the cup is full. The tea begins to spill onto the lacquered tray, overflowing on the richly embroidered carpet. "Stop," cries out the king, "my cup is full." "Indeed," replies the teacher, "and the full cup can receive no tea." With those words, the teacher bows and leaves the courtroom. The full cup can receive no tea. That is the message the king is left to ponder. This is no less the message of these teachings of Jeshu. Our natural condition is so ego filled that it has little space for spiritual teaching of any kind. Yet, to follow the path that will later be described more fully by Jeshu, one has to have room. One has to be an empty cup.

4 The second beatitude, much like the first, has to do with receptivity. To mourn is to have space for the sorrow of others. This refers not only to personal sorrows but to planetary ones as well. To mourn is to feel the loss that occurs when our environment deteriorates, when rage replaces reason in society, when war becomes the normal means of conflict resolution. It takes room to mourn for all the sorrow and loss in our world today.

5 The third beatitude speaks of gentleness, a rare commodity in our violent world. Gentleness should not be confused with weakness. It has the strength of water, the resiliency of wind. This teaching asserts that it is the gentle who really possess the earth. A Chinese proverb claims that the ocean is the greatest body of water because it lies the lowest. It is this lowly condition that enables it to receive all the waters of the earth. Humility, too, means to be close to the earth. Those who walk gently on the earth are its truest owners.

6 An extraneous reward lessens the integrity and sublimity of the act. So, too, the reward in heaven that is promised to those walking this

(continued on page 32)

You're successful if you know how to mourn; God will comfort you.[4] You're successful if you're gentle; you'll inherit God's earth.[5] You're successful if you're starving to be God-centered; God will satisfy you fully. You're successful if you're compassionate to others; God will be compassionate to you. You're successful if your purpose is always pure; you'll see God. You're successful if you work for peace; you'll be called God's children. You're successful if you're persecuted for being God-centered; God's reign is yours. You're successful if people insult you, persecute you, and slander you on my account. Be happy! Be glad! Your reward[6] is great where God reigns. Remember that the same things happened to the prophets who lived before you.

(continued on page 33)

path consists of existing at that higher level of consciousness that is called heaven. The reward of being more fully human and, therefore, more God-centered is the abundant life that flows from being more fully human, more God-centered.

Anyone counting these blessings or promises of success comes up with nine; and yet, intuitively we might expect seven—the perfect mystical number, the number of days in the week, and the number of Christian sacraments. In a treatise St. Augustine wrote near the end of the fourth century called *The Lord's Sermon on the Mount,* he finds seven beatitudes and regards the final blessings regarding persecution as recapitulation, especially since, like the first beatitude, they promise God's reign. I see those final references to persecution as stemming from the experience of the early community and not from Jeshu himself. And so by a different route than Augustine's, I come back to the idea of an original seven.

7 In the opening verses of this chapter we are told that it is Jeshu's disciples who gather around him to hear his teachings when he goes up the mountain. It is clear that they are the intended audience for this teaching, since the example of salt flavoring and preserving food implies a relatively small agent, the salt, and a relatively large object, the food. This suggests the relative size either of Jeshu's community of disciples to the larger society of his day or of Matthew's community in the context of the more extended environment in which it existed.

8 How can salt lose its saltiness? Salt was a very basic and extremely important commodity. Our word *salary* (from the Latin word for salt, *sals*) takes us back to a time when wages were paid in blocks of salt. Because it was so precious, poor people would sometimes dilute it with fine sand, thus stretching it to last longer. After a certain point, however, the saltiness would be so diluted that the substance became worthless, except as something to be scattered on the beaten path to one's door. So too, the special savor of a God-centered life can become so diluted as to have no efficacious influence on the larger society.

"You are the salt[7] of the earth, but if salt were to lose its saltiness,[8] what could restore its flavor? It would then be good for nothing except to be thrown out on the road.

(continued on page 35)

⚠ Scholars refer to the early Christian communities as house churches, since the members of the community could often meet in one person's home. Matthew's community, for example, may have consisted of no more than some fifty to sixty people who were able to meet together in a large home belonging to one of the members, possibly in the city of Antioch. On the other hand, we may be dealing with several such communities scattered throughout Syria. In either case, we are dealing with relatively small numbers. Such minority groups can easily be understood as a seasoning to the larger society.

9 The example of the lamp suggests outreach. In this case, a tiny lamp can bring light to an entire one-room house. Many of these ancient lamps are unearthed by archaeologists today, and it is easy to see how they can be extinguished simply by placing a bowl over them. It makes no sense to light one of these lamps and then immediately extinguish it. It should be placed on a table to illuminate the room. Using this illustration from ordinary life, the disciples are told that they too should let their light shine.

10 The light from the lamp refers to the disciples' good works, just as the lamp indicates the faith from which those good works spring—that is, a trust in God's reign and the possibility of experiencing it, however provisionally, in the here and now. Faith and works are brought together here in an understandable way. By trusting God—not as old man in the sky but as our own ground of being—we find the resource (the lamp) to live that trust in outreach (the light) to our neighbor through deeds of love and compassion.

⚠ These reflections bring us to the central premise of all these teachings. God's reign, that is, the whole of reality centered in God, already floods Jeshu's consciousness. The sense of what a God-centered life meant before the disobedience of Adam and Eve, the sense of what a God-centered life will mean when humankind reaches a plane of authentic spiritual existence—this provides the white-hot center of Jeshu's consciousness. If we are able to turn from our ego-dominated

(continued on page 36)

"You are the light of the world. A city built on a hill can't be hidden. We don't light lamps[9] and then immediately extinguish them; we put them on lampstands so that they can provide light for everyone in the room. In just this same way, your light[10] should shine so brightly for others that they can both see your good works and praise your heavenly Parent.

(*continued on page 37*)

lives and trust the reality of God's reign, then we will begin to experience it ourselves. Jeshu's disciples can already taste and touch in him the reign of God that for most people remains a distant horizon—either removed in the mythological past of the primordial paradise or distant in the eschatological promise of a transformed world.

11 Matthew's community of believers consisted primarily of Jews like himself, though there were undoubtedly a few Gentile converts. These Gentiles, however, took on a fully observant Jewish life, exceeding even the Pharisees in their observance. In other words, the community probably continued to practice circumcision and observe the dietary laws (kashrut), along with other holiness codes familiar to those members who had grown up as Jews. It is important to keep in mind that these people continued to see themselves as Jews, indeed as the "true Israel." Matthew's community was still grasping the slender hope that their model of Judaism would become the normative one for all Jews. But since it was largely Gentiles and not Jews who were eventually attracted to the community, the result was that, within less than a century, Christianity became a largely Gentile enterprise.

12 Words are almost physical things in their power to hurt or heal. Young people teased at school become the murderers of their classmates. It is not only the manifestation of anger in physical abuse that is to be avoided; the hateful mindset itself delivers a harmful blow to our neighbor. Angry thoughts and angry words (insults or curses) bring us to the judgment of the community and ultimately to the judgment of God.

13 Consider the text about leaving one's offering at the altar until one has been reconciled with the estranged neighbor. Some years ago I spoke with an African priest whose parish was a rural village. He told me that every Saturday a straw is passed from home to home in the village. In presenting the straw to one's neighbors, one must be reconciled with them and able to embrace them in a spirit of true peace. If the straw is returned to the priest by Saturday evening, then the Sunday

(continued on page 38)

"Don't think that I've come to discard the Torah and the Prophets. I have not come to discard but to complete.[11] Until this present universe passes away, not the smallest letter or even one stroke on a letter will be removed from the Torah until everything written there comes to pass. The one failing to fulfill even the least of the *mitzvot* and teaching others to do the same will be called least in God's reign. But the observer of these *mitzvot* who teaches others to do the same will be called the greatest in God's reign. For unless your God-centeredness exceeds that of the Torah scholars and Pharisees, you'll never enter God's reign.

"You've heard how it was said to people long ago, 'You shall not murder; and whoever murders shall be brought to trial.' And now I tell you that whoever is angry with a fellow human being shall be brought to trial, whoever insults a person will answer to the Sanhedrin, and whoever says to someone 'God damn you!' deserves a hell of fire.[12] So if you are about to bring your offering to the altar[13] and remember that a fellow human being has something against you, leave your offering there and go home. After you're reconciled with that other person, then come back and offer your gift. If someone sues you, try to reach an agreement before the case comes to court, or you may be brought before the judge, then turned over to the police, and finally put in jail, where I promise you won't get out until you've paid your last cent.

(*continued on page 39*)

service proceeds as usual with a communion. However, if the straw is not returned to the priest, then presumably some of the villagers were unable to settle their differences. In that case, the Sunday liturgy has no communion, and the whole community is called to heal its divisions.

14   As with anger, so it is with adultery. The rabbis taught that there is an adultery committed with the eyes as well as the adultery done with one's whole body. We are called to pay attention to our thoughts and words as well as to our deeds. These teachings coalesce in mindfulness. Jeshu reinforces the importance of this theme in his dramatic, frankly outlandish language about plucking out our right eye or cutting off our right hand. Since most people were prejudiced against what was "left" (like our "left-handed compliment") and biased toward what was "right" (the God-centered sit at God's "right hand"), this emphasis on the right eye and the right hand seems to point up our natural inclination—our normal prejudices, if you will. They represent our habitual consciousness, the automatic pilot by which our lives are usually steered. What we are being asked to do, then, is to change that prejudice, reorient that natural inclination, and center ourselves in the reality of God's reign.

This collection of teachings goes beyond external deeds to intentionality. They highlight Jeshu's role as a teacher of *kavanah*. Rabbi Abraham Joshua Heschel speaks of the delicate balance of Jewish life in terms of *keva* and *kavanah*. *Keva* is the principle of regularity manifested in the things one does as an observant Jew. *Kavanah* is the power of spontaneity manifested by one's intention in performing a mitzvah, one's attention to inwardness while completing the outward deed. Heschel sees a healthy Jewish life—and indeed any kind of healthy spirituality—as a balance of these two elements. Too much *keva* and one ends up with what Heschel calls pan-halachism, a form of religion incapable of seeing beyond external observance. Too much *kavanah*, however, and one falls into another distortion, a feeling-based religiosity that has no rootedness in actual deeds. The secret, as in so much of spirituality, is in the balance of these two realities.

"You've heard the commandment not to commit adultery.[14] And now I tell you that the man who looks at a woman and starts making plans to sleep with her has already committed adultery with her in his heart. If your right eye is an occasion of sin, pluck it out and throw it away. It's better to lose one eye than to have your whole body thrown into hell. And if it's your right hand that is the occasion of sin, cut it off and throw it away. It's better to lose one limb than to have your whole body thrown into hell.

(continued on page 41)

15 Whether we are talking about inflicting injury on our fellow human beings, participating in public worship, or dealing with potential civil suits, the teachings call us to an attentiveness to the inner situation. This emphasis appears most strikingly in the teachings regarding marriage. Jeshu knows that divorce is allowed by Jewish halacha, or law, but that is not the perspective from which he views the relationship between a man and a woman. He is looking at these committed relationships from the perspective of God's reign. He wants his audience to be aware of the inner reality of this relationship as well as its legal and societal status.

16 If you ask someone to verify his or her statement by taking an oath, you imply that the person's word may not be reliable enough unless it is accompanied by some kind of verbal guarantee. Jeshu asks his disciples to begin thinking about the way we live from the viewpoint of higher consciousness. By refusing to take oaths, one refuses to accept as normative a world in which people lie and in which you are unwilling to believe others except reluctantly when they are under oath. In other words, one helps to call into being a world where people can be trusted to be truth tellers.

17 The teaching of "an eye for an eye and a tooth for a tooth" is probably one of the most misunderstood teachings in scripture. It is often used to contrast the supposedly vengeful teaching of the Jews with the merciful teachings of Jeshu, thereby setting up the "Old Testament" with its harsh and angry God as a foil for the "New Testament" with its God of love and mercy. Such an approach displays a vast ignorance of both the Hebrew Bible and the Christian Testament. The two aspects of the divine mystery, justice and compassion, are visible in both scriptural collections. The Hebrew scriptures are filled with stories of God's compassion, just as the Christian writings contain numerous passages filled with rage and vengeance.

The teaching of Jeshu here is not a condemnation of the Torah teaching but a development in another direction. As Mahatma Gandhi commented, "Where the law is eye for eye, everyone ends up blind."

(continued on page 42)

"It has also been said that any husband divorcing his wife should give her an official notice. And now I tell you that the husband who divorces his wife, except in the case of her unfaithfulness, is guilty of making her commit adultery if she marries again, and the man marrying such a woman commits adultery as well.**15**

"You've also heard how it was said to people in the past: 'Don't perjure yourself; perform whatever you have sworn in the sight of the Lord.' And now I tell you not to swear at all.**16** Not by heaven, since that's God's throne, nor by the earth, since that's God's footstool, and not by Jerusalem, since that's God's city. Don't even swear by your head, since you can't make a single white hair black. Just say 'yes' or 'no'; anything more than that stems from the Evil One.

"You've heard it said 'An eye for an eye and a tooth for a tooth.'**17**

(continued on page 43)

That would certainly be true if the law were to be taken literally. A study of these texts and the rabbinic commentaries surrounding them clarifies that this represents a teaching of mercy, one describing a principle of limitation. Not long ago, in England, someone could be hanged for shooting one of the king's deer. This teaching, by contrast, insists that any punishment be proportionate to the crime.

18 So if we don't go toe to toe with the other person, what do we do? Do we let ourselves become a doormat? Some translations tell us not to resist evil, but the Greek verb implies more of a militant response. We should resist evil. The question is, how? What Jeshu proposes outlines a hardheaded strategy—admittedly risky but a strategy nevertheless. A strategy for what? For the transformation of consciousness. Whose transformation? The other whom we are not choosing to categorize as enemy, but whom we are trying to love into a relationship of equality. We don't love others by letting them disrespect us, even when superior power is theirs.

19 Turning your face after the first slap is a strategy for redefining the context of the meeting. The slap with the back of the hand (therefore, a slap to your right cheek) is a contemptuous gesture, reflecting a disparity of power and position. Turning your left cheek necessitates that the other person hit you with an open palm, and this is a gesture reflecting equality of status. So what Jeshu recommends here is not an act of weakness but a strategy for facilitating a possible breakthrough in the consciousness of the one who slaps you.

And now I tell you not to go toe to toe with the person doing evil to you.[18] If anyone slaps the right side of your face, let that person slap the left side as well.[19]

(continued on page 45)

20 Giving your shirt to someone who has already taken your coat leaves you naked. And who would be taking these items of clothing in the life-world from which this text springs? The Romans who are turning poor Jews out on the streets, often after displacing them from their peasant holdings so that imperial building projects can flourish. How can the Jews protest this injustice? Jeshu does not recommend a militant response. But every Jew seeing you naked would recall the great prophet Isaiah, who walked naked through the streets of Jerusalem for three years as a sign of the injustices of the government. Perhaps this startling strategy would motivate other Jews in their peaceful resistance to the Roman tyranny.

21 Luke omits the teaching about the extra mile, possibly because its anti-Roman attitude is all too evident to the Gentile evangelist of the Roman Empire. At this time, Roman soldiers could conscript any Jew to carry their gear for one mile. So during that first mile, the oppressed person is defined by the relationship of conqueror to conquered. But what if the Jew then offers to carry the Roman soldier's gear for a second mile? This is not stupidity but strategy. The Jewish peasant has redefined the situation. If during the first mile he was a slave, during the second mile he carries the burden as the Roman soldier's equal. Might this lead to some change in the attitude and/or behavior of the Roman? It is at least possible.

Have not these teachings been used to oppress the weak? Very definitely so, but only when they are misunderstood. The old Latin motto *Corruptio optimi pessima* tells us that the corruption of the best things is the worst kind of corruption. Even spiritual teachings can become weapons of abuse. That is precisely why it is so important to understand that these teachings are not about powerlessness but power, not about weakness but strength, not about victimization but control. They are strategies for achieving a more God-centered world through nonviolent strategies of confrontation.

And if someone takes you to court to sue you for your shirt, let that person have your coat as well.[20] And if someone forces you to carry his gear one mile, carry it two miles.[21]

(continued on page 47)

22 Giving to people in need, lending without collateral or calculation—these kinds of activities deny any sense of ultimate ownership. The Psalmist tells us that the earth is the Lord's, and Leviticus reminds us that we are tenants on God's land. The whole sense of individual ownership—symbolized by our gated communities, our home security systems, and our panic rooms—stands in sharp contrast to the world Jeshu describes, one that is more reflective of a consciousness before fences were built to separate what is mine from what is yours.

Few people embodied the spirit of Jeshu more than the thirteenth-century saint of Assisi, Francis. The motto he gave to the brothers who gathered around him in community was *Meus et tuus non habitant in domo nostro:* "Mine and yours do not live in our house."

23 Hating one's enemy is not found as a command in the Hebrew scriptures, but the injunction occurs with great frequency in the writings of the Essenes found among the Dead Sea Scrolls. Perhaps this qualifies as one more indication that Jeshu may have spent some time with this sect. But whether or not Jeshu was an Essene for a while, this command moves us to the very highest kind of spiritual consciousness. Enemies are precisely those people we should hate. Asking us to love our enemies is asking us not to have enemies. It challenges us to move beyond the dualistic world divided into friends and enemies into the world God sees, a world where all of us are brothers and sisters.

24 It is easy to be nice to one's friends. Jeshu raises the bar considerably. Our love should reach out to all people, just like the sun and rain in their indiscriminate gift to humankind. The thirteenth-century theologian and saint Thomas Aquinas tells us that love is *velle bonum alterius,* willing the good of the other. This has nothing to do with our likes and dislikes, our attractions or repulsions. We are to will the good of all those with whom we come in contact. In this way we become perfect as our heavenly Parent is perfect.

25 I used to fear the word *perfect,* seeing in it an impossible ideal. But when I first read this passage in German, I noticed that the word was

(continued on page 48)

"When people ask you for something, give it to them; when they want to borrow something, lend it to them.[22] You've heard it said: 'Love your neighbor and hate your enemy.' But what I am telling you is to love your enemies and pray for your persecutors.[23] This is how you will become children of your heavenly Parent, who lets his sun come up for bad and good people alike, just as he sends rain both to those who are God-centered and those who are not. What's to your credit in loving just your friends?[24] Don't even the tax-collectors do that? And if you say hello only to your own people, have you done anything extraordinary? Don't even the Gentiles do as much? You should grow to your fullness, becoming whole and holy, like your heavenly Parent.[25]

(continued on page 49)

vollkommen, a clear cognate to the English phrase "to come full." We are to come full, like the rose in its fullness or the full moon, like the full-faced smile of a baby or the full fruit ripened on the vine. God is the fullness of existence, and we are called to be fully all that we have the capacity to be. Jeshu's call is to a full and abundant life.

26 This language about reward may seem confusing. Is Jeshu really appealing to some external reward for our good behavior? One has to keep in mind his Jewish tradition, in which the rabbis remind us that "the reward of the mitzvah is the mitzvah"—the reward of doing a good deed is the good deed itself. The reward of the heavenly Parent "who sees all secrets" is nothing less than our own full and abundant life in God's Spirit. Ultimately life has no greater reward than a rewarding life.

27 "Pious phonies" miss the mark because they fail to see beyond their religious "duties" to the deeper matters of the spirit. The external exists to facilitate the internal. We create a false dichotomy by believing we must choose between one or the other. Both can be there, but the challenge is to use the external guidelines as a means to the internal reality, eventually knowing when to let go of them.

⚭ This material on almsgiving, prayer (with the exception of the Lord's Prayer), and fasting are peculiar to Matthew. These three categories of observance suggest a certain level of community development. Almsgiving implies living beyond the subsistence level oneself and thus having something to give to those in need. Community prayer implies stability, since ordinarily a regular place and time are both required for community prayer to take place. Fasting presumes relatively normal eating habits, so that one can decide to limit the intake of food on a given day. All of these conditions might be more applicable to Matthew's community than to Jeshu and his disciples, who more likely received alms than gave them. Their prayer together could hardly have been bound to regular times or places. And they more than likely ate gratefully whenever they had food to eat, fasting more by circumstance than by choice.

"Don't parade around showing off your God-centered deeds; if you do, you can forget about any reward[26] from your heavenly Parent. When you make a charitable donation, don't blow a horn first like the pious phonies[27] you see sometimes in places of worship, or even in public, who are out to win the praise of other people. Believe me, they have their reward. But when you make a charitable donation, don't even let your left hand know what your right hand is doing. That's how secret your giving should be. Then your heavenly Parent, who sees all secrets, will reward you.

(*continued on page 51*)

28 The Lord's Prayer is the one part of this passage that has a parallel in Luke. One of the petitions, however, is in Matthew alone: the prayer that God's will may be done on earth as in heaven. Since parallelism is the most common mark of biblical poetry, one can certainly understand this petition as restating the one that precedes it: the prayer that God's reign might come. In that case, we see an excellent definition of what God's reign is all about, since the doing of God's will on earth with that same totality with which God's will is done in heaven (presumably by the angels) would certainly mean that God's reign had come. We see both the here-and-now dimension of the prayer as well as its eschatological, or end-time, orientation. We also see the dynamic meaning of God's reign, not as a place but as a state of reality in which life is centered in God.

29 Meister Eckhart, a fourteenth-century mystic, calls our attention to one of the phrases of the Lord's Prayer. When we ask for "our bread" rather than "my bread," we are already acknowledging that the bread belongs to all of us. We read in one of Eckhart's sermons: "Whoever does not give to another what belongs to the other, such a one does not eat his own bread but eats the bread of another along with his own." In a very real sense, giving to someone in need is recognizing the other's right to have what already belongs to that person.

30 What is forgiveness? Forgiveness offers future. When we forgive another person, we do not deny what that person has done to hurt or offend us, nor do we forget it (despite the popular phrase "to forgive and forget"). What we do, however, is offer that person future—the possibility of changing, of being different. When we make a mistake, we want that option for ourselves, so it only makes sense that we offer it to others. God is the one who can most offer us future, no matter what we have done in the past. But God's hands are tied if we fail to manifest that same attitude toward others. Even God cannot offer future to someone who offers no future to fellow human beings.

"When you pray, don't be like the pious phonies who love to make a show in places of worship and in public so that everyone can see them. Believe me, they have their reward. You need to be able to pray to your heavenly Parent in secret in your room with the door shut. Then your heavenly Parent, who sees all secrets, will reward you. When you pray, don't babble on endlessly like the Gentiles, who think that their wordiness will guarantee an answer from God. Don't imitate people like that. Your heavenly Parent knows what you need before you even ask.

"This is how you should pray: Our heavenly Parent, may your Name be made holy. May your reign come and your will be done, on earth as in heaven.[28] Give us today our[29] bread for the coming day. Forgive us our failings, as we forgive those who fail us. Don't let us be tested beyond our strength, and save us from every evil.

"If you forgive[30] the failings of others, your heavenly Parent will forgive you, but if you're unforgiving toward others, your heavenly Parent will be unforgiving toward you. When you fast, don't put on a glum face as the pious phonies do. They go so far as to neglect their appearance so that others will notice that they are fasting. Believe me, they have their reward. But when you fast, groom your hair and wash your face so that others won't even know that you are fasting. But your heavenly Parent, who sees all secrets, will know you are fasting, and he will reward you.

(continued on page 53)

31 Most of what people treasure is susceptible to rust, moths, and thieves. Jeshu calls his disciples to reflect on the things they treasure, leading them to recognize what treasure it is that truly captures their heart. If our house were on fire, what would we make the first effort to save? Our loved ones? Our portfolios and cash boxes? Our art works and jewelry? This process leads us to recognize what Paul Tillich called our ultimate concern. It's another name for our greatest treasure, and that in turn is another name for our god. Jeshu invites us to conclude that what most deserves worship as our god is indeed none other than God.

32 The teaching is about our eye, not our eyes. The two physical eyes are not the focus here; Jeshu is referring to what Hindus call the third eye, the center of wisdom. And wisdom is more than knowledge or information; it brings all these disparate elements together into a single field of vision. Spiritual wisdom should illuminate and unify all that we are and do. It is the one clear light proceeding from our third eye that keeps all of our life whole, thus ensuring that our entire body is illumined.

☯ There is a parallel to this text about the eye in the teachings of Fa-yen Wen-i (885–958 c.e.), the founder of the Chinese House of Fa-yen. He spoke of a single eye, which he called the dharma eye (Fa-yen) or the Tao eye. He once asked his monks: "When the 'eye' [the channel] of a wellspring gets stuck, it is because it is filled up with sand. Now, when the Tao eye is not opened, what is obstructing it?" When his monks were unable to answer his question, Fa-yen answered it himself: "The obstruction lies in the eye!" Everything that we know is disclosed in our consciousness; nothing in our awareness lies outside the borders of that same consciousness. So if that consciousness is somehow blocked or obstructed, "filled up with sand," then the water of pure consciousness cannot flow.

33 If we live with awareness, then we realize that we cannot serve two masters; in other words, we cannot sustain two ultimate loyalties. Paul Tillich's theology of an ultimate concern was no mere academic nicety.

(continued on page 54)

Don't pile up treasures on earth, where moth and rust take their toll and thieves break in to steal. Lay up your treasures in heaven, where neither moth nor rust can do them harm and thieves will find nothing to steal. For your heart will always be wherever you keep what you treasure.[31]

"The eye[32] is the body's light. If it's healthy, the whole body will be illumined, but if it's diseased, the whole body will be in darkness. And if the light in you is dark, what a darkness that will be! You can't serve two masters at once.[33] You'll either hate one and love the other or be loyal to one and despise the other.

(continued on page 55)

He experienced his fellow Germans falling into idolatry, investing with ultimacy something not deserving of it. Tillich exposed the idolatry at the heart of the Nazi ideology. He realized that he could not have Hitler as his leader (Führer), since only God could make that claim on him. Only a muddied consciousness can try to live with two masters, two ultimate concerns, two gods.

34 The teaching does not say that we cannot *have* wealth and serve God. It says rather that we cannot *serve* both God and wealth. Jeshu gives abundant examples of being overly concerned about matters that are not ultimate. They may deserve an appropriate level of concern, but they do not merit our final loyalty. The examples are powerful and seem as appropriate today as in the life-world of the first century: what we will eat, drink, or wear.

35 This teaching does not promote vagrancy. We can make plans for next year. We can take out insurance policies and sign mortgages. We can register in degree programs and plant gardens. The operative idea here is not that we don't *think* about these things but that we don't *worry* about them. Worrying adds to the picture a lack of trust in God and a lack of honesty about the nature of all human plans. As one Buddhist teacher reminds us, our ideas about possible futures should be plans, not demands. And a Yiddish proverb tells us that what makes God laugh is our plans.

36 Where is our center? This question burns at the core of Jeshu's teachings. If God's reign has captured our heart of hearts, if God's reign is our most precious treasure, then everything else will find its rightful place in our lives. Our center dictates and determines all the rest of our choices. We may need to prepare for tomorrow, but we do not need to be all worked up about tomorrow. It is today that merits our most exquisite attention, for today is the reality where God's reign can best be known and experienced.

You can't serve both God and wealth.[34] That's why I tell you that you shouldn't be overly concerned about what you'll eat or drink or wear. Aren't you more than your food and your clothes? Look at all the birds flying around in the sky. They neither farm nor fill barns, and yet your heavenly Parent provides nourishment for them. Aren't you worth more than those birds? Does all your worrying[35] really add anything to your life? And why be overly concerned about your clothes? Look at how the wildflowers grow without working to make clothes for themselves. Believe me, not even Solomon in all his splendor could match the beauty of even one of those flowers.

"If God provides nourishment for the weeds that we see today and throw on the fire tomorrow, will that same God not provide for you despite your lack of trust? So don't be preoccupied with your food and clothes. The Gentiles fret enough about all those things. Remember that you have a heavenly Parent, who knows all your needs. Make your first concern God's reign and a God-centered life, and then let God handle all those other needs. Don't be all worked up[36] about tomorrow. Let tomorrow worry about tomorrow. You've got enough to concern you today.

(continued on page 57)

37 There is an inward realm where each of us can be judged only by God. Here it is imperative that we relinquish any right to pass judgment, for we ourselves will fall under the same judgment with which we judge others. This mirrors, of course, the petition in the Lord's Prayer in which we ask that our failings be forgiven to the same extent that we are willing to forgive the failings of others. *Sinner* is a word we can use only in the first person.

Whenever I teach this text, the same question generally arises in one or another form: "What about Hitler or Bin Laden? Can't we even judge them?" "No," I reply, "at least not on this matter of their internal dealings with God." Again, we have to remember that Jeshu is a teacher of *kavanah*. There is no problem with a policeman arresting someone for running a red light, with a judge finding a criminal guilty, or even with a parent sending a misbehaving child to its room. In all those cases we are judging external behavior, and no society could function without our ability to make judgments of those kinds. It's the judgment of the heart that must be left to the only One who intimately knows the human heart.

38 The image of the speck of dust and the log is a delightful example of the hyperbole so typical of the Middle East that was the life-world both of Jeshu and of the authors of this gospel. The parables and aphorisms of Jeshu ripple with peasant humor, but our solemn mode of reading these texts "from the pulpit" seldom leads to laughter. We nitpick at others so easily while ignoring great gaps in our own halos. The image of any one of us examining a speck of dust in our neighbor's eye while ignoring the log protruding from our own is both funny and uncomfortably close to the truth.

39 These images of dogs being given the sacred meat of the Temple sacrifices and pigs stomping on pearls seem extreme. We know that "pigs" and "dogs" formed part of an accepted code in the Jewish world for talking about Gentiles, especially the hated Romans. But would Jeshu have indulged in this kind of ethnocentrism? If so, it is an

(continued on page 58)

"Don't judge,[37] or you will be judged, and the same standard will be used to judge you that you use in judging others. How is it that you're so alert at finding a speck of dust[38] in the eye of your neighbor and yet take no notice at all of the log in your own eye? You pious phony! Take the log out of your own eye first, and then you'll see well enough to remove the speck of dust from the eye of your neighbor. Don't give what is holy to dogs, and don't throw pearls in front of pigs—they'll only stomp on them and then turn on you.[39]

(continued on page 59)

example of how Jeshu himself had to grow beyond some of the ethnic prejudice that characterized his inherited life and language.

It's important to realize that this teaching is not found in either of Matthew's sources, namely, Mark or Q. Did our present text originate with Matthew's pen? If so, what is it really saying? Is it a criticism of the kind of outreach to Gentiles represented by the Pauline communities in which no adherence to halacha, Jewish law, was required of Gentile members? It may well be that we are hearing Matthew's voice in this passage rather than the voice of Jeshu.

40 These verses about asking, seeking, and knocking bring us back to the profound level of spiritual teaching exhibited in the earlier verses of this chapter. The importance of prayer, heartfelt and urgent prayer, appears here as it does in many of the great spiritual traditions. The nineteenth-century Bengali saint Sri Ramakrishna is quoted as saying, "Cry to the Lord with an intensely yearning heart, and you will certainly see Him." How important it is that our prayer be heartfelt, sincere, from the very center of our being. Such prayer reaches the heart of the Divine.

41 In talking about God's unqualified goodwill toward us, Jeshu again uses humorous examples, this time to illustrate how silly it is to imagine parents giving their children stones or snakes instead of bread and fish.

During my early years as a Jesuit, my novice master gave a talk in which he told us that God was like a mother bird filling the mouths of her young with as much food as they could hold. "The wider they open their mouths," he said, "the more food she gives them. There are limits to the baby bird's capacity but never to the mother's generosity." An apt image for the loving Father/Mother God described here in Jeshu's teachings.

"Ask and you'll receive; seek and you'll find; knock and the door will be opened to you. For those who ask will receive; those who seek will find; those who knock will have the door opened for them.**40** If you are a parent whose children are asking for bread, will you give them stones instead? Or if they're asking for fish, will you give them snakes? If you, limited as you are, know how to give your children what is good for them, how much more will your heavenly Parent give good things to those who ask?**41**

(continued on page 61)

42 The so-called Golden Rule is commonplace in the world's religious literature. It is one of those striking insights that can powerfully illumine our everyday choices. "Would I like to be treated like that?" "Would I want someone to say that to me?" We have to remember, however, that what I want for myself may not be what my neighbor wants. If I enjoy Beethoven's music, I might conclude that taking my neighbor to a Beethoven symphony would be the best of birthday presents. If, however, my neighbor listens only to rap music, it will probably not be a successful evening. It's not a matter of doing what I want done to me but of doing whatever is done in the way I would like it to be done to me.

43 The teaching about the narrow gate is often understood as referring primarily to the number of people who will end up in hell. I find an entirely different intent in this teaching—namely, that people must go through a narrow gate one at a time. That is how all spiritual progress must be made. We can find support in a community or guidance in a director, but any walking of the path belongs uniquely to each of us as an individual pilgrim on this earth. A mob can move toward destruction, but only an individual can choose life.

44 The text tells us that most people choose to enter by the wide gate, which is the easy option, but not many choose the narrow gate, which is the hard path. Does this not justify the interpretation that most people are going to hell? First of all, one must recognize that this passage comes from Q and reads quite differently in Luke 13:23–24. There, someone asks whether those who are saved will be few. Instead of answering the question, Jeshu urges his interlocutor to strive to enter by the narrow door, since many will seek to enter it and not be able to do so. In other words, do not worry about others' practice; be concerned about your own.

Treat others the way you want them to treat you.[42] That's what the Torah and the Prophets are all about. "Enter through the narrow gate,[43] for the wide gate and the easy path[44] lead to destruction, though most people choose to enter that way. But it's the narrow gate and the hard path that lead to life, and there aren't many who find it.

(continued on page 63)

45 There is a shorter version of this Q saying in Luke 6:46. There, Jeshu asks why some people call him "Lord, Lord" and yet do not do what he teaches. Here in Matthew, the teaching speaks of prophecies, exorcisms, and miracles. Yet, these extraordinary deeds have no value if they lead to Torah violations. People may have all these powers and yet be "doers of lawlessness." The voice we hear may be that of Matthew and his community, where observance of the Torah remains a requirement of true discipleship. For the author of this gospel, no amount of charismatic activity replaces obedience to the Torah, just as no amount of pretty leaves on a fruit tree makes up for its lack of good and edible fruit.

46 The final image of the two houses also stems from Q. It makes intuitive sense that the foundation is important for any project undertaken. I once saw a house slide into a valley in Mexico because, as I was told by my friend, the foundation had been poorly laid. The beginning is everything—whether in architecture, education, or the spiritual life.

47 The last verse of the teaching, the capstone to the first of the five collections of teaching materials in Matthew, tells us something very important about Jeshu. The majority of teachers are people who work close to a text. This is the role of a rabbi, explicating the text that has been received in the community. The great spiritual adepts, however, are more than teachers, more even than prophets. They simply declare the ways things are at that level of ultimacy we recognize as divine. They do not have to quote chapter and verse like teachers or even state that they are speaking God's word like prophets. They simply lay claim to the authority to articulate what most deeply characterizes human existence.

"Look out for phony prophets, who are like hungry wolves coming to you in the skins of sheep. You'll know them by their fruits. Do you pick grapes from thornbushes or figs from thistles? Healthy trees bear good fruit, just as withered trees bear fruit that is worthless. A healthy tree never bears worthless fruit any more than a withered tree bears good fruit. And trees not bearing good fruit are cut down and thrown into the fire. That's what I meant by saying that you will know them by their fruits. Not everyone who says to me, 'Lord, Lord' will enter where God reigns, but only those who do the will of my heavenly Parent. In that final day there will be many people calling out, 'Lord, Lord, didn't we prophesy in your name? Didn't we cast out demons in your name? Didn't we perform many miracles in your name?' But I will tell them openly, 'You were never friends of mine, so get away from me now, for your deeds are far from what is taught in the Torah.'[45]

"Those who hear my teachings and act accordingly are like wise people who built their houses on a rock foundation. When the rains and the floods and the winds came, those houses held up because they were built solidly on rock. Those who hear my teachings and don't act accordingly are like foolish people who built their houses on sand. When the rains and the floods and the winds came, those houses collapsed—and what a collapse that was!"[46] When Jeshu had finished these teachings, the crowd was amazed at the way he taught. For unlike the Torah scholars, he taught with authority.[47]

1 The Sermon on the Mount is the largest body of teachings attributed to Jeshu anywhere in the Christian Testament. When Moses came down from the mountain with the Ten Commandments, he found a world of riotous chaos and idolatry. Now when Jeshu descends from the mountain, he encounters a world of suffering and sin. Perhaps Matthew was thinking of Jeshu's teachings on the mountain as a new understanding of the Ten Commandments, because he proceeds to present us with ten miracle stories.

⚛ The world Jeshu now enters is much like the world from which the Buddha's father wanted to protect his royal son; and yet, as with Jeshu, it was precisely through seeing this world that the young prince embarked on his spiritual quest. Unlike the Buddha, however, Jeshu had not grown up in a palace. His life was never protected from the hard realities of peasant existence: hunger and homelessness, sickness and death, oppression and persecution. Now Jeshu enters this world in a new way, not as its victim but as its healer.

2 One must read chapter 13 of Leviticus to get some sense of the legislation involving these severe skin diseases. In verses 45 and 46 of that chapter we are told that people with such a leprous disease must walk around calling out "Unclean, unclean" so that others know to avoid them. So when Jeshu touched the leper, he rendered himself *tameh*, ritually impure. Such impurity does not imply a moral fault or sin, but it is nonetheless a serious violation of the holiness code that is vitally important in the life-world of Jeshu and of any observant Jew.

3 Did a skin disease dramatically and instantaneously disappear from a man's body one day near a hillside in the Galilee? I do not know, nor does anyone else. I have no problem in accepting the possibility of a spontaneous healing, but that is not really the point. It was clearly not the mission of Jeshu to cure all the skin disease in the land. These stories of healing occur in the context of deep personal encounters. When Jeshu heals, he also empowers. He leads people to the realization that their lives should move toward wholeness and healing at every level

(continued on page 66)

3 □ Coming Down from the Mountain (Matthew 8:1-9:38)

Large numbers of people crowded around Jeshu, following him as he came down from the mountain.[1] A leper[2] stepped forward, knelt before him, and said, "Lord, if you want to, you can heal me." Reaching out his hand, Jeshu touched him and said, "Of course I want to. Be healed."[3] Immediately the man's leprosy disappeared.

(continued on page 67)

of their being. What cannot be doubted is that Jeshu was a healing presence.

4 The completely unselfconscious way in which Jeshu lives within his Jewish world can easily be missed in this story. He sends the cured leper to the proper priestly authorities, adhering to the prescriptions of that same thirteenth chapter of Leviticus alluded to in note 2. Jeshu can cut through the many-layered grid of the socialized world, for he sees this leper as God's child, someone created in God's image. And yet, Jeshu knows full well what it is for this man to have to live and function in his social milieu. Thus, he wants the leper's healing to be corroborated by the validation of the priests.

5 Jeshu deals loosely with religion but tightly with God. He does not reflect the anxious scrupulosity and obsessive concern that so often characterizes people who are really "into" religion. Nor does he seem to be possessed by a passionate need to reject religion as an insidious enemy of human freedom and creativity. Religion is there, and it has a role to play. Thus, in meeting this Roman officer, who presumably adheres to the civil religion of Rome with its pantheon of gods and goddesses, Jeshu makes no effort to convert him. Nor does he attempt to engage him in a religious conversation. He simply meets him as one man to another and attends to his needs.

6 The level of this officer's trust in Jeshu's power to heal is even more remarkable than his sensitivity to Jeshu's Jewishness. This Roman officer has lived among Jews long enough to know that they have religious concerns about entering a Gentile home. The statues of the gods of the family and nation, the presence of ritually improper foods—these and other such "pagan" elements might make an observant Jew less than comfortable. This officer sees no need for Jeshu to enter his home and thus have to deal with these potentially contaminating elements. As a commander of men himself, he knows that he has only to issue an order for a result to take place at some distance. Why should not this

(continued on page 68)

Jeshu then said to him: "Don't talk about this to anyone until you have submitted yourself to a priestly examination and offered the sacrifice Moses commanded.[4] Then your witness will be valid for everyone."

When Jeshu came into the city of Kapharnahum, a Roman officer came to him,[5] asking for his aid. "Lord," he said, "my boy is laid up at home, paralyzed and in a great deal of pain." Jeshu replied, "I will come and make him better." But the officer remonstrated: "I am not worthy, Lord, to receive you in my house. If you just say the word, my boy will be healed. I am a man used to authority, with soldiers under my command. They come and go when I say the word; they do things because I give the orders." When Jeshu heard this, he was amazed, and, turning to the people around him, he said, "Believe me, I've not found this kind of trust[6] among my fellow Jews.

(continued on page 69)

hasid, this Jewish holy man, be capable of the same kind of exercise of authority? No wonder Jeshu stands amazed at this level of trust.

7 Praising the officer's depth of trust seems in order, but why the vehement denunciation of Jewish unbelief? The whole direction of the story is thereby shifted from praise of the Gentile's faith to a diatribe against the Jews. Not only is there a dramatic vision of inclusive Gentile participation at the end-time banquet ("many people are going to come from east and west"), but there is a deliberate exclusion of the people for whom the banquet was originally intended.

Essentially, the same story occurs in Luke 7:1–10. Both evangelists, therefore, seem to be drawing on a common source. There are two significant differences in Matthew's telling of the story. First, he fails to include the verses in Luke that praise this officer as one who loved the Jewish people and built their synagogue for them. Second, Matthew seems to go beyond the narrative's framework to contrast this faithful Gentile with unfaithful Israel. This gives a harshly judgmental tone to the end of the story in Matthew—something totally lacking in Luke's version.

Most critical scholars see this part of the story as stemming from a life-world later than that of Jeshu. It is only after a history of painful rejection and even hostility that a community of Christians would be moved to such a harsh judgment of their contemporaries. Matthew's community has parted company with Judaism, though there may still be some hope that even if Israel has been rejected by God, individual Jews will be converted.

8 Jeshu heals Rock's mother-in-law, prompting the neighbors to show up on her doorstep that evening with all the sick people in the neighborhood. Jeshu sends out healing in all directions, and Matthew uses the occasion to quote a verse from Isaiah that teaches vicarious suffering—that is, how one person can suffer for another. This is the only place in Matthew where we find explicit mention of this chapter of Isaiah, and it is interesting that it is used here in a context of Jeshu's

(continued on page 70)

I've got to tell you that many people are going to come from east and west to sit down at table with Abraham, Isaac, and Jacob where God reigns, but the children called to that reign will be thrown outside into the darkness, where they will weep and grind their teeth in despair."[7] Then Jeshu said to the officer, "Go home now. Everything will happen just as you trusted it would." And the boy was cured at that very moment.

Jeshu then went into Rock's house, where he found Rock's mother-in-law burning up with fever. He touched her hand, and the fever disappeared. She immediately got up and began to wait on him. When it was evening, neighbors brought to Jeshu many persons who were possessed, and simply by giving a command, he expelled the evil spirits and healed all those who were sick. In this way the oracle of the prophet Isaiah was fulfilled: "He took our infirmities upon himself and carried all our illnesses."[8]

(continued on page 71)

healings rather than in the context of his sufferings. Jeshu is clearly presented as being deeply involved with humankind in its suffering and pain, somehow taking it on as his own.

9 The two men in this story are a study in contrasts. The first is too eager; the second too hesitant. The first exudes naïve enthusiasm; the second a penchant for making excuses. Jeshu reminds the first man, a student of Torah, to ponder the commitment he is making in such a cavalier fashion. He challenges his willingness to embrace his own radically itinerant lifestyle.

10 The point of Jeshu's response to the second man, one who is already a disciple, is not to deny the propriety of burying one's parents or even attending to their needs as they approach death. Jeshu addresses the hesitancy in the man's commitment, a hesitancy cloaked in the garb of filial duty. Thus, Jeshu's somewhat explosive answer attempts to pull away the curtain of rationalizations behind which this man is hiding.

11 There is no rational way of explaining the comment about the dead burying their dead. Who are these "dead" being left to bury others? Perhaps the phrase is best understood as one of those Middle Eastern hyperboles, like camels squeezing through needles and logs in people's eyes. Rather than answering the man's objection, Jeshu may be dismissing it as a rationalization unworthy of a serious answer, while at the same time trying to focus this disciple's attention on the step that he needs to take—the real challenge of the moment.

We are not told what either of these men decided to do after these challenging responses on the part of Jeshu. This may in the last analysis be a parable about the cost of discipleship, inserted by Matthew to show us that true discipleship lies between two extremes. Too much initial enthusiasm may lead to burnout. Too much excuse making may prevent effective decision making. Following the path of discipleship entails avoiding both of these dangers.

When Jeshu saw how large the crowds were, he told his disciples to go to the other side of the lake. At that point a Torah scholar came up to him and said, "Teacher, I am ready to follow you wherever you are going."[9] "The foxes have their dens," Jeshu replied, "and the birds have their nests, but I have nowhere even to lay my head." Then someone who was one of his disciples said to him, "Lord, let me go home first and bury my father."[10] "You just follow me," Jeshu replied, "and let the dead bury their own dead."[11]

(continued on page 73)

12 Having seen Jeshu's power over disease, we now are shown how he can control the forces of nature. The picture painted here is impressive but probably not factual. We recall the story of the Buddha coming to a stream and meeting a holy man who tells him that after years of meditation he is able to walk on water to cross the stream. The Buddha asks him why he expended so much energy attaining this power when he could have easily crossed the stream at any time by giving a nickel to the ferryman. A magical event of this kind is best understood as a parable of Jeshu's power to calm the troubled waters of human fear and anxiety.

13 Few tears would be shed by a Jewish audience on hearing this story, since pigs were unclean animals that should be neither eaten nor raised. Their dramatic demise would occasion more humor than regret. While many of us might find it bizarre that Jeshu would literally send demons into pigs, it is certainly plausible that he was healing two hysterical men, while some pig farmers failed to notice that their herd, disturbed by the violence, had stampeded in the opposite direction. In the long run, the loss of their livestock outweighed meeting a holy man, and they drove Jeshu out of town. This mentality matches our own, where bottom-line considerations so easily outweigh spiritual opportunities.

14 The text speaks of Jeshu's "own city" in this story, undoubtedly referring to Kaphernahum, the Galilean hub of Jeshu's activities.

15 In most instances of healing, Jeshu speaks to the person's trust in God. In this case, however, it is not the paralytic's trust that Jeshu recognizes but the trust of those who are carrying him. This detail serves to highlight the corporate character of human existence: the fact that we are not isolated atoms in this divine drama. In a very real sense, we carry one another about, either to greater healing or to greater dis-ease.

16 What is this forgiveness of sins of which Jeshu speaks? The word for *sin* in both its Greek and Hebrew forms means to "miss the mark,"

(continued on page 74)

Jeshu climbed into the boat, then, and his disciples followed him. A huge storm blew up suddenly on the lake so that the waves were almost capsizing the boat, and yet Jeshu was lying there asleep. His disciples came and shook him awake, crying out, "Lord, save us or we'll drown." But Jeshu just said to them, "Why are you frightened and so lacking in trust?" Then Jeshu stood up in the boat and commanded winds and waves alike, and there was a great calm. The disciples asked in amazement, "What kind of a man is this that even the winds and the waves listen to him?"[12]

They arrived at the other shore, in the neighborhood of the Gadarenes, and there Jeshu encountered two possessed men who clambered out of some nearby tombs. They were so fierce that no one dared to use the road that ran by there. At once they cried out, "What do you want with us, Son of God? Have you come here to torment us before the appointed time?" Now there was a large herd of pigs feeding not far away from there, and the demons begged Jeshu, "If you're going to cast us out, send us into that herd of pigs." Jeshu said to them, "Go ahead!" The demons then went out of the two men and entered the pigs, and with that, the whole herd of pigs plummeted down the hillside into the lake water, where they drowned. The pig farmers ran away to the nearby town and told everyone what had happened to the two possessed men. Then the townspeople came to meet Jeshu, and when they found him, they asked him to leave their territory.[13]

Jeshu took the boat back across the lake and came to his own city,[14] where some people brought him a paralyzed man lying on a stretcher. Jeshu recognized the trust of the people who carried the paralyzed man to him,[15] and he said to him, "Have courage, son, your sins are forgiven."[16]

(continued on page 75)

an apt image for our efforts to center our self-identity on the eccentric ego, which is wide of the mark and off target, instead of moving toward that bull's-eye where our self is concentric with the Divine. As with all aspects of healing, this forgiveness of sins is not so much done *for* us by Jeshu as done *through* us when we allow ourselves to be open to God's reign. Jeshu reminds us of the expansiveness of God's love and acceptance while encouraging us to trust it. As we trust that flow of divine love and compassion we are empowered to stop clinging to the ego, thereby allowing ourselves to stream toward the depths of the divine reality.

⚠ Sin is not something positive, but a lack or dramatic absence. Sin is a "wound in being"; and a wound is not something added to our body but the separation of tissue that belongs together. Sin, then, is a kind of rupture of being, a failure to love—to will the fullest reality for ourselves and others. It is a failure to trust—to have faith in the expansiveness of God's reign and reality. Taoists would say that it is a failure to notice that the universe, like a piece of wood, has a grain and that all our woodworking must respect that grain.

17 The story closes with the awe that the onlookers feel in witnessing Jeshu's exercise of authority. Just as the earlier collection of sayings ended with a statement about the authority of Jeshu's teachings, here we find a testimony to the authority of Jeshu's deeds. Commanding the forces of nature, subduing wind and water, controlling the powers of the nether world, casting out demons and devils, subduing the debilitating forces that attack physical health and wholeness—in every case of life springing out of control, Jeshu can and does exercise divine authority.

18 We come now to the meeting from which this gospel's name is derived, although the phrase "according to Matthew" was added to the text several decades after its composition. The tax-collector who only in this gospel is called Matthew (Mattiyah in our translation) is known as Levi in the parallel stories in Mark and Luke. Mattiyah (Levi)

(continued on page 76)

Hearing this, some of the Torah scholars standing around said to one another, "This is blasphemy!" Jeshu, however, knowing them inside out, said to them, "Why do you fill your minds with so much evil? Do you think it's easier to tell him that his sins are forgiven or to tell him to get up and walk? Just so that you know I have authority on earth to forgive sins (here he spoke to the paralytic): "Get up now; take your stretcher and go home." And the former paralytic did just that. The people watching all this were overwhelmed with a sense of awe, and they praised God for giving this kind of authority[17] to human beings.

Moving on from there, Jeshu saw a man named Mattiyah[18] sitting at a tax-collector's station, and he said to him, "Follow me." Mattiyah stood right up and followed him.

(*continued on page 77*)

responds to Jeshu's compelling charisma and in one leap moves from tax-collector to disciple.

19 The Romans were clever to use Jews as tax-collectors for their fellow Jews. These employees of the Empire were required to reach the quota required by Rome but were free to keep whatever exceeded that quota. It is not surprising, therefore, that most Jews did not associate with these "collaborators," who were generally not known for their punctiliousness in religious observance. Thus the objections of the Pharisees to Jeshu's open sense of table fellowship with people of their kind.

20 The whole scene, whether factual or not, provides a context for one of Jeshu's central teachings. Like the Buddha, Jeshu embodies a message that alleviates suffering and promotes healing. One wonders, however, whether he is being serious when he talks about religious people who do not need his services. The standard Christian interpretation has always been that since all are sinners, any presumption of God-centeredness apart from Jeshu is fallacious. On the other hand, perhaps Jeshu really does recognize the possibility of people who are religiously healthy, just as there are people who are physically well. After all, he seems to know nothing of what later theologians would speak of as original sin: an inherent alienation from the Divine.

21 The next exchange seems to reflect the life-world of Matthew much more than that of Jeshu. Three things seem clear. First, Jeshu and his disciples did not observe regular times of fasting. Their wandering lifestyle, as well as their poverty, more than likely militated against this. Second, the followers of Jochanan did observe regular times of fasting. Third, the members of Matthew's community did observe regular times of fasting. This reference to Jeshu as bridegroom probably derives from Matthew's life-world (in other words, this is more the way the community came to think about Jeshu than the way he thought about himself), and the passage in its present form explains both why the community fasts regularly now and why Jeshu and his disciples did not have such regular fasts.

Later, when Jeshu was having dinner inside, many tax-collectors and people lax in Torah observance joined him and his disciples at the table.[19] Seeing this, some Pharisees said to his disciples, "Why does your teacher eat with tax-collectors and unobservant Jews?" Overhearing this question, Jeshu said to them: "It's not the strong and healthy who need a doctor, but the sick and infirm.[20] Go and find out what the passage in scripture means that says, 'I want compassion, not animal sacrifice.' For I have come for the unobservant, not for those who are properly religious."

Then Jochanan's disciples came to Jeshu and asked, "Why is it that your disciples don't fast,[21] when we and the Pharisees fast so often?" Jeshu replied, "Do you expect the friends of the groom at a wedding dinner to be sad while the groom is still with them? The time will come soon enough when the groom is taken away from them, and then they will fast.

(*continued on page 79*)

22 The whole business of old patches on new cloth and old wineskins and new wine is intriguing. What was Jeshu saying? Certainly not that he wished to establish a new religion. He knew enough of the dangerous tendency toward self-idolatry in all religious structures. He may, however, have wanted to clarify that those joining his *chavura,* his group of disciples, must understand that something new is being announced. God's reign is breaking through all the traditional restraints of society and religion. Jeshu offers his followers a new and heady wine that cannot be contained by the old order.

23 I never felt the significance of this story until I was talking about this passage to a Jewish adult education group at a nearby synagogue. As I read the standard English translation I could hear various people saying the word *tzitzit.* That day I realized how much better prepared a Jewish group is to understand some aspects of the gospel than a comparable Christian group. It is so easy to forget that Matthew is itself a midrash on the Hebrew Bible and that the whole story derives its meaning from the Jewish milieu in which it arose.

The *tallit,* or prayer shawl, continues to be worn by Jews and is the sartorial ancestor of the stole often used today in liturgical contexts by many ministers and priests. The *tzitzit* are the fringes of the *tallit.* We read about them in Numbers 15:38, where Moses is told to command the Israelites to make fringes on the corners of their garments. In Numbers 15:39 it is stated: "You have the fringe so that, when you see it, you will remember all the *mitzvot* of the Lord and do them...." The *tallit* with its *tzitzit* highlights Jeshu's Jewishness, something all too often ignored in Christian iconography and imagination. Wearing the *tallit* signified being wrapped in God's Torah.

When the woman touched Jeshu's *tzitzit,* far more was involved than simply touching the hem of his garment. She was touching something that symbolized God and God's commandments, something holy. This sharpens the contrast with her uncleanness. In Leviticus 15:19–28, we read that a woman with a discharge of blood is *tameh,* ritually unclean, and communicates that ritual uncleanness to anything or

(continued on page 80)

"No one uses a piece of new cloth to patch up an old coat.[22] The patch would just tear away from the coat, and the hole would be bigger than ever. By the same token, you don't put new wine that's still fermenting into old winebags. If you did, the brittle winebags would burst open, spilling the wine and ruining the winebags as well. When you have new wine, you put it into new winebags, and then both are kept safe."

While Jeshu was in the midst of these teachings, an official came to him, and kneeling at his feet, pleaded, "My daughter has just died, but if you were to come and touch her with your hand, she would live again." So Jeshu and his disciples got up from the table and followed the man home. While they were on the way, a woman who had been suffering from hemorrhages for twelve years came up behind Jeshu and touched his *tzitzit*.[23] She was thinking that if she could just touch his *tzitzit* she would be healed. Turning around, Jeshu saw her and said, "Have courage, my daughter, your trust has brought you healing." And from that moment on, the woman was well.

(continued on page 81)

anyone she touches. Jeshu, however, does not complain about uncleanness; he simply assures her that her trust has brought her healing, and the flow of blood ceases.

24 Mark's gospel (5:21) identifies this official as a synagogue president named Jairus, but in copying this story Matthew omits that detail—one more example of his negative feelings toward the rabbinic Jews and their synagogues in his life-world of the late 80s.

25 The funeral is in progress when they arrive, and Jeshu makes a puzzling comment about the little girl simply being asleep. Why does he say this? Jeshu lives at a deeper center of consciousness, beyond the rigidity of so many of our dualistic conceits. We tend to lock on to our categories and cling to our definitions with such finality. But when we look more deeply at play and work, death and sleep, black and white, we realize that they dance far too close to one another for our comfort. Jeshu moves in our world but is not totally of it. For him, death turns to life again as easily as the movement from sleep to wakefulness.

⚠ This story needs to be read against the richly textured narratives of the Hebrew Bible. Early in our story, we saw that Jeshu was three times David. Repeatedly, we have seen how he walks in the footsteps of Moses. Now he seems to wear the mantle of the great prophet Elijah and his disciple/successor Elisha. In I Kings 17:17–24, Elijah took the dead body of a widow's son to the upper chamber where he was staying. There he prayed to God for the child's life, and God "listened to the voice of Elijah; the life of the child came into him again, and he revived." In II Kings 4:17–37, we read of a similar story in which Elisha raised a dead boy and returned him to his mother. With models such as these, Jeshu can surely do no less. Jeshu is a life-bringer, a life-restorer. Of that there can be no doubt.

After this Jeshu arrived at the official's house,[24] where he went inside and found the musicians there for the funeral and people mourning loudly. Jeshu told them to get out, saying that the little girl had not died but was only sleeping.[25] They just laughed at him. But when the crowd was finally dismissed, Jeshu went into the room, took the little girl by the hand, and she got up. It wasn't long before this story had spread all around that region.

(continued on page 83)

26 What I most like in the story of the two blind men is that Jeshu explicitly asks them whether or not they trust his ability to restore their sight. Clearly, this demonstrates the necessity of their involvement in this process. To make the point even more explicit, Jeshu prays, in the very act of opening their eyes, that this be done according to their level of trust. How big are the borders of trust? Jeshu seems to want to know this about the people he meets.

27 Why this stress on secrecy, especially when no one ever seems to obey Jeshu on this point anyway? Is this simply something inherited from Matthew's sources? Is this because of Jeshu's fears that people will misunderstand his mission, thinking that he has come to seek fame as a worker of wonders?

28 Why do the Pharisees so persistently misjudge Jeshu's healing and life-giving presence? These are largely straw men Matthew has created, the enemies of Matthew's message in those later years of the first century, when it was becoming all too clear that few Jews were accepting what Matthew's community offered.

29 This series of ten healing stories ends with the picture of Jeshu filled with compassion for the crowds who were harassed and helpless, like sheep without a shepherd. Then the image shifts to a field ready for harvest and the need to pray for disciples who would labor against all odds to bring God's harvest home.

As Jeshu was moving on from that place, two blind men walked behind him, crying out, "Son of David, show us compassion!" These blind men came up to Jeshu after he had gone inside the house. Jeshu said to them, "Do you really trust that I can do this?" They replied, "Yes, Lord."[26] So Jeshu touched their eyes and said, "May everything happen just as you have trusted." With that, their eyes were opened. Jeshu then admonished them very sternly not to tell this story to anyone.[27] But they were no sooner out of the house than they were telling the story all over town.

When these men had left, someone was brought to Jeshu who was mute and possessed with a devil. Jeshu cast out the devil, and the man who had been mute talked again. The crowds said in amazement that nothing like this had ever been seen in Israel. But some Pharisees[28] there claimed that Jeshu was casting out devils in the name of the Prince of Devils.

Jeshu continued through all the towns and villages, teaching in their synagogues, announcing the good news of God's reign, and healing every kind of disease and illness. And whenever he looked at the crowds of people around him, he was filled with compassion[29] for them, since he recognized how worried and anxious they were, like sheep without a shepherd. At one point, Jeshu said to his disciples: "How rich is this harvest and how few the workers. You must ask the owner of these fields to send workers out for the harvesting."

1 The first thing that would strike anyone reading this passage is the explicit exclusion of non-Jews from the mission of the twelve, a detail omitted in the Marcan and Lucan parallels. If one jumps ahead to the end of the gospel, one sees that these instructions contradict what Jeshu tells his disciples after his resurrection. Presuming that the author of the gospel was as aware of this contradiction as we are, the only conclusion seems to be that the text presupposes a mission whose directives changed after the resurrection. In other words, Jeshu originally envisages a mission to his fellow Jews, a form of Jewish renewal. When this movement fails because of Jewish resistance and rejection, then the post-Easter Lord countermands this limitation and sends his disciples to all the nations, Jews and Gentiles alike.

2 Can we salvage anything here of some directives that Jeshu might have given to his own disciples? Yes, especially if we use Mark as our guide for reading Matthew. Clearly, Jeshu did have a purpose, and he had disciples as well—people who were called to share his mission. What was that mission? To embody God's reign by being a healing presence in the world, just as Jeshu was. This entailed eschewing all the trappings of power and wealth belonging to Caesar's reign. It clearly demanded a higher consciousness than that of the empire-obsessed Romans.

4 □ Choosing Disciples to Share in the Work (Matthew 10:1-11:1)

Jeshu called his twelve disciples to himself and gave them authority to cast out unclean spirits and to heal every kind of disease and illness. The names of those twelve apostles are as follows: first, Shimon (called "Rock") and his brother Andri; the sons of Zebedee, Jacob and his brother Jochanan; Philip; Bar-Tolmai; Toma; Mattiyah, the tax-collector; Jacob, the son of Chalfai; Taddai; Shimon the Zealot; and the traitor, Judah Iscariot.

It is these twelve that Jeshu sent out after giving them the following instructions: "Don't go into the territory of the Gentiles nor into any Samaritan towns.[1] Go rather to the lost sheep that belong to the house of Israel. And announce to people along your way that God's reign is very close to them. Heal the sick, raise the dead, cleanse the lepers, drive out the demons.[2] Give away free of charge all that has been given to you free of charge. Don't bring along wallets full of gold, silver, or copper coins, or even a clothes bag or an extra set of clothes, not even sandals or staff. A worker deserves to be supported.

"When you come to a town or village, find a suitable host and stay with that person until you leave. When you enter the house, extend to it your peace. If the house is suitable, your greeting of peace will rest there; if the house is not suitable, your greeting of peace will return to you. And if some house or town does not welcome you or listen to you, get out of there, shaking its dust from your feet. Believe me when I tell you that Sodom and Gomorrah will fare better on judgment day than the places that reject you.

(continued on page 87)

3 A later history is described here: the life-world of Matthew's community in the late 80s. Matthew's Jeshu previews the hostile response Matthew's community will receive from both Jews and Gentiles. This demonstrates once again that the gospel often teaches us more about its life-world than Jeshu's. Hostility will be heightened as zealous Jewish leaders call the Jewish adherents of the Jesus movement to accountability in synagogue courts. And leaders of this movement, people like the authors of this gospel, respond with bitter reprisals. They begin to shape their own story with an increasingly anti-Jewish spin. Eventually, as this story grows and develops legs outside the community, it will become full-blown anti-Semitism.

⚛ It is important to see Jeshu's message against the prevailing message of the Roman Empire. The so-called Pax Romana (Roman peace) was one imposed by Roman power and maintained for the economic and political well-being of the Romans. The peace Jeshu proclaimed, biblical shalom, was a fullness of life stemming from the establishment of justice in the world and from a participation in a God-centered life. Jeshu's message was meant to attract people, not to coerce them, and what it promised was not economic benefit but life.

4 The teachings about hidden things being revealed, spoken in the light of day, and proclaimed from rooftops seem consonant with Jeshu's message, especially when understood in an existential context—understood, in other words, not as literal realities but as poetic descriptions of the human condition. Everything already exists under the sign of death and the seal of eternity. Nothing is really hidden, secret, or whispered. Our whole being in the world is disclosure and revelation. We act and speak in the sight of the angels. Either we manifest what is real, deep, and eternal, or we are liars.

5 The teaching concerning all that can harm us suggests that we not get too caught up in what affects us superficially, paying attention instead to what can damage us eternally, in terms of our deepest reality before God. Jeshu is obliquely referring to the power of the Roman

(continued on page 88)

"See how I am sending you out like sheep among wolves. You've got to be wary like snakes and yet innocent like doves. Be on your guard! Your enemies will drag you into courts, flog you in their synagogues, haul you before governors and kings—all on my account and so that you can witness both to them and to the Gentiles.[3] And when you are handed over in this way, don't be overconcerned about what you're going to say or how you're going to say it. Words will be given to you when the time comes. It won't really even be you who are speaking then, but the spirit of your heavenly Parent will be speaking in you. Brothers and sisters will be turning each other in to be killed; parents will be doing the same thing with their own children, just as the children will turn against their parents to have them put to death. Because of me, you will be hated by everyone. Nevertheless, those who hold out to the end will be saved.

"If they persecute you in one town, run off to the next one. Believe me when I tell you this: I will come in glory before your work in the towns of Israel is finished. Disciples aren't greater than their teachers, nor are slaves above their masters. It's enough for disciples to be treated like their teachers and slaves like their master. If they have called the head of the house Beelzebul, they will certainly do nothing less to the members of the family.

"It's important that you not be afraid, for there is nothing hidden[4] that will not be revealed, nothing secret that will not be made known. What I tell you under cover of darkness, you are to speak out in the light of day. What has been whispered in your ears, you are to proclaim from the rooftops. Don't be afraid of those who can kill your body but are unable to harm your deeper reality.[5] Fear only the one who has the power to destroy all of what you are in hell.

(continued on page 89)

Empire, whose minions could indeed enslave, torture, and crucify. And yet, horrible as all those realities are, they do not touch what lies deepest in a human being. From this faith the martyr's confidence is born. And it is the blood of martyrs that proves to be the seed of faith.

6 The teaching about sparrows, pennies, and the hairs on our head breathes the earthiness of Jeshu too much to have any other source. At the same time, these teachings reveal the profoundly mystical tenor of Jeshu's worldview. These words come from the heart of someone who recognizes that the divine reality throbs in every detail of our experienced world. We learn two lessons of tremendous importance: God knows, and God cares. But what about God's power to change things?

When Rabbi Abraham Joshua Heschel was asked where God was at Auschwitz, he said that it was the wrong question and that we should be asking where human beings were at that time and place. In other words, we should not blame God for the messes we make through our own ignorant choices. God really did leave it up to us to finish the garden world in which we were placed, to create the world of justice and peace of which God dreams. A more scientific way of saying this is that after our genetic evolution essentially ended some forty thousand years ago, evolution moved to consciousness; and we thus became conscious and responsible for our further evolution.

7 Although words of Jeshu may underlie some of these verses, for the most part they bear the signature of Matthew. We see an organized community making distinctions: the community's founder, prophets within the community, its God-centered members, and those who are the very least within its parameters. The community's corporate ego emerges when we are told that giving someone in need a drink of cold water is not enough; it must be done because that person is a disciple of Jeshu. The plants of religious intolerance are already taking root in the soil of Matthew's gospel.

"Can't you buy a couple of sparrows for a few cents? And yet it is impossible for one of them to fall to the ground without your heavenly Parent's knowledge—why, even the hairs on your head are all counted.[6] So don't be afraid; you're worth a lot more than a whole flock of sparrows! People who publicly stand up for me, I will stand up for in the presence of my heavenly Parent; but people who publicly deny me, I will deny in the presence of my heavenly Parent.

"Don't think that I've come to bring the world an easy peace. What I bring is much more like warfare than that kind of peace. My coming sets sons against fathers, daughters against mothers, daughters-in-law against mothers-in-law. You won't have to look beyond your own family members to find your enemies. You're not worthy to be my disciple if you prefer father or mother to me; you're not worthy to be my disciple if you prefer son or daughter to me; you're not worthy to be my disciple if you're not ready to take up your cross and follow me. If you try to cling to your life, you will lose it. It's only by letting go of your life for my sake that you can really possess it.

"When people welcome you, they're welcoming me; and when they welcome me, they're welcoming the one who sent me. Whoever welcomes prophets because they are prophets receives the reward of prophets. And whoever receives God-centered people because they are God-centered receives the reward of the God-centered. Believe me when I tell you that anyone who gives even a drink of cold water to the least of my disciples and does it because that person is my disciple, such a one will not go unrewarded."[7] When Jeshu finished instructing his twelve disciples, he left that place to teach and preach in the towns of Israel.

1 The visit of Jochanan's disciples provides Jeshu with an occasion to say something to the people around him about his former mentor. Jochanan is God's messenger without equal; he is Elijah returned; he is the greatest human being to be born of woman. It would be difficult to imagine any higher praise that Jeshu could give to the prophet now languishing in prison, and yet his answer delineates an unbridgeable chasm between two worlds, two epochs of salvation history, and, perhaps more important, two ways of understanding God's reign.

2 The world of Jochanan remains a world in which God's reign is conceived as a dramatic and violent breakthrough of God's power into human history, reversing the current order of Roman domination and exalting the oppressed Jews. The popular conception of God's reign is still "on the perpendicular," a divine meteor falling on the fault line of human history, the "ax to the tree" of which Jochanan spoke so powerfully. This remains a favorite trope for shouting televangelists, promising a sweet revenge when the godless fall into the hands of a wrathful God.

3 What is this whole business of God's reign being under attack? Who are these attackers who are making every effort to seize it? Jeshu changed his idea of God's reign sometime after Jochanan's arrest. He realized that a mere role reversal of Jews and Romans would change too little. Would Jewish power really be an improvement over Roman power? Not unless a more radical transformation was achieved. So far, Jews were too much like their Roman masters in seeing God's reign in terms of the power of domination. Even Jochanan envisaged God's reign as a time of divine revenge, bringing violence to those who had perpetrated violence. Jeshu realized that the whole conversation about God's reign had heretofore been saturated in a commentary of violence. Now that was all going to change.

5 ☐ Criticism Follows a Man of Controversy (Matthew 11:2-12:50)

Jochanan, who was in prison, had been hearing about all that the Messiah was doing; and he sent two of his disciples[1] to ask Jeshu whether he was the one they had been waiting for or whether they should be looking for someone else. When Jeshu heard this, his response was: "Go back and tell Jochanan what your own ears and eyes witness: blind people see and the lame walk; lepers are cured and deaf people hear; the dead are raised back to life and poor people listen to good news. You're on the right track if all these things I'm doing don't upset you."

When Jochanan's disciples had left, Jeshu spoke to the crowds around him: "What was it you expected to see when you went out into the desert? A hollow reed blown about by every wind? What did you really go out to see? Someone dressed up in expensive clothes? You'll find that kind of person in a mansion. So what were you really looking for? A prophet? Yes, a prophet. And I would add—much more than a prophet. This is the person scripture talks about: 'Look how I am sending my messenger ahead of you to prepare your way.' Believe me when I tell you that no woman has ever given birth to a greater human being than Jochanan the Immerser. And yet the least important person in God's reign is greater than Jochanan.

"From Jochanan's time[2] until today, God's reign has been subjected to violence,[3] and the violent have claimed it.

(continued on page 93)

4 The text as we have it reflects a later perspective. Jochanan was Jeshu's Elijah, the prophet who did not die because he was taken up to heaven in a fiery chariot, the one who would return to precede the Messiah. But beneath this later commentary we glimpse teachings that come from Jeshu himself. A new era is dawning. Part of the reason that Jochanan belongs to the old era lies in the fact that he, like so many others at that time, was caught up in a vision of role reversal and vengeance. Jeshu, however, will teach that Jews—and indeed all human beings—need to accept a different kind of God consciousness, entailing a different sense of power. Jeshu will proclaim not power as domination but power as service and love.

5 The roles of Jeshu and Jochanan are different but complementary. Their distinct ministries represent two eras, one culminating in Jochanan and the other beginning in the ministry of Jeshu. Both speak for God's wisdom, a wisdom that we are reminded in the final verse of this passage can be revealed only by what actually happens. Jochanan enunciates that wisdom in an ascetic form, and he is labeled demon possessed. Jeshu exhibits that wisdom through a lifestyle of open-table fellowship, and he is deemed too loose and nonobservant. What kind of tune can wisdom play if neither rap nor Rachmaninoff pleases the crowd?

6 What does this new understanding of God's reign entail? Surely this calls us to let go of any desire to see our enemies (including those we see as God's enemies) "get theirs." We are all on the same path, growing in the same direction. The Buddha nature arises in the worst of criminals; the Christ consciousness grows in the worst of sinners. God's reign is a world without enemies or "bad guys." This does not eliminate the necessity of controlling and containing certain behaviors for the common good and for the protection of the rights of others. But controlling does not have to mean branding as evil. It is judgment that we need to relinquish, the judging of others as sinners, the separating of "deserving" and "undeserving" poor, the pretense of knowing who is and who is not on God's side. Our primary goal should be to hear

(continued on page 94)

For until you come to Jochanan, all of the scriptures are prophecy. And if you're ready to accept that prophecy, you know that Jochanan is the Elijah whose return the scriptures promise. Those of you who are ready for this teaching will understand it.[4]

"But let me now try to find a comparison for the rest of my contemporaries. They're like the children you see around the marketplace who call out to their playmates: 'We played a happy tune, and you didn't want to dance; we played a sad tune, and you didn't want to make long faces.'[5] For when Jochanan came eating and drinking hardly anything, people said that he was possessed by a demon. But then I came along eating and drinking freely, and the same people accused me of being a glutton and a drunkard, a friend of tax-collectors and the unobservant. Nevertheless, God's wisdom will be revealed in the end by what actually happens."[6]

Then Jeshu began to denounce the towns where he had done most of his powerful deeds because these towns had not undergone a change of heart. "You're in for hard times, Korazin, and you too, Beit-Tzaidah. For if the powerful deeds done in you had taken place in Tyre and Sidon they would long ago have put on sackcloth and ashes as a sign that they had undergone a change of heart. It's going to be a lot better for Tyre and Sidon on judgment day than for you. And you, Kapharnahum—do you hope to be lifted up high as heaven? You will be brought down as low as hell, for Sodom itself would still be a thriving city today if it had experienced the powerful deeds you have known. And you can be sure that it's going to be a lot better for Sodom on judgment day than for you."

(continued on page 95)

and act on that call of wisdom, however it reaches our ears. For it is what actually happens that matters most in the end.

7 Perhaps this passage, a paean to the intimate relationship between the Divine Child and the heavenly Parent, was a source of consolation for the early Christian missionaries who experienced resistance from many of those in their social world who were regarded as wise and educated leaders. By contrast, they themselves were the simple folks, God's poor, God's blessed ones. What they are blessed with exceeds all earthly treasure, for they are blessed with an intimate relationship with God that would have been unavailable if it had not been offered by the one who enjoys sole and privileged access to that very divine life.

8 The "yoke of the Torah" was a common trope in Jewish teaching. Certainly everyone in Matthew's audience knew that the way of Torah faithfulness was often described through this image of a yoke, a common farm implement typically worn by two animals. The root of this word takes us back to the ancient word *yoga,* something that links us to the divine reality. Now we hear of another yoke, another yoga. And for the members of Matthew's community, the yoke of the new law proclaimed by Jeshu is less burdensome than the yoke of Torah taught by the Pharisees, the later rabbis of Matthew's time.

⚮ A common liturgical prayer, the "Gloria," contains a thrice-repeated *Tu Solus* phrase. The words mean "you alone." Accompanied by the right music, the phrases can be thunderous in majesty: "You alone are holy; you alone are Lord; you alone are most high." We find the same kind of exuberant and exclusivist language in this section of Matthew. Only this Divine Child can mediate a relationship to the heavenly Parent. Words like these are a besetting problem for biblical literalists, though they have always been understood by poets, mystics, and lovers. Within any good relationship the connection tends to be felt as unique, as indeed it is. We give lovers the permission to say, "I have just met the most gorgeous man on the planet." Divine lovers need that same kind of leeway. Dogmas and doctrines carve this kind of

(continued on page 96)

At that time Jeshu said, "I thank you, heavenly Parent, Sovereign of heaven and earth, that you have revealed to simple folks what you have kept from the clever and educated. And yet, heavenly Parent, that seems to be how you in your goodness choose to do things. Everything has been entrusted to me by my heavenly Parent, and no one enjoys full intimacy with the Child except the Parent, just as no one enjoys full intimacy with the Parent except the Child, and those to whom the Child wants to reveal that Parent.[7]

Come here, all of you who feel as if you're carrying the world on your shoulders, and I'll lighten your load. Take my yoke[8] on your shoulders and learn from me, because I'm gentle and humble of heart. You'll find rest for your souls, for my yoke is easy to bear and my burden is light to carry."

(continued on page 97)

arrogance in stone. "Jeshu is the only way to the Father." "No one can be saved except through Jeshu."

9 Jeshu's disciples are accused of plucking grain to satisfy their hunger as they walk through some wheat fields on a Sabbath. This action does not involve a clear violation of halacha, or Jewish law, and is therefore a doubtful matter, one that is open to varying interpretations. The Dead Sea Scrolls provide us with a text in which we see that Essene halacha allows for picking grain on the Sabbath and eating it, as long as the person does not carry any away. But the ordinary pharisaic halacha did not allow this exception.

10 The twofold argument presented by Jeshu revolves around both what rabbinic discussion calls a *hekish,* a parallel situation, and the application of *kal v'chomer,* a principle that operates much like our *a fortiori*—what is sauce for the goose is certainly sauce for the gander. In other words, if David could violate a holiness code in a case of definite infringement, then Jeshu's disciples can do the same in a case of doubtful infringement. The second illustration regarding the way cultic activities supersede Sabbath observance operates in much the same way.

11 Whether or not Jeshu ever said that he was greater than the Temple or called himself Lord of the Sabbath, he probably acted with a sense of authority and implied that he thought of himself that way. This might well have been in a context, however, in which Jeshu regarded every human being as greater than the Temple and Lord of the Sabbath. A great deal depends on how mystical a consciousness we attribute to Jeshu. Was God so deeply his reality that everything else was really God in another form, God manifested in matter, God embodied in humanness?

Around this same time, Jeshu and his disciples were walking through some wheat fields on the Sabbath. Being hungry, the disciples were picking the tops of the grain to eat.[9] Some Pharisees saw this and said to Jeshu, "Look at your disciples; they're guilty of violating the Sabbath." He replied, "Haven't you read what David did when he and his companions were hungry? Going into God's house, David ate the special loaves kept there in God's presence, bread that neither he nor his companions had the right to eat, since they were reserved for the priests.[10]

"Or haven't you read in the Torah how the priests in the Temple regularly violate the Sabbath and yet are without guilt? Are you aware that someone greater than the Temple is here? If you understood the scriptures that tell us how God wants compassion more than ritual sacrifice, you wouldn't be condemning people who are without guilt. For it is the Lord of the Sabbath[11] who is here with you."

(continued on page 99)

[12] The scene described in this passage shows Jeshu once again acting with authority. He enters a synagogue and heals a man with a crippled hand, despite the challenge by the ever-present Pharisees. As with the example of plucking grain, we are in an area of halachic controversy. Saving a life justifies violating Sabbath observance. The point here, however, is that a man with a crippled hand can certainly wait until sunset to be healed.

[13] In using the example of pulling the sheep out of the pit, Jeshu seems to be speaking with a humorous irony. He is also employing *kal v'chomer* once again. In other words, Jeshu is telling them that the sheer potential economic loss of a farm animal might well motivate them not to be so punctilious about this disputed area of halacha (that is the irony). And yet, if they are willing to make an exception for an animal in trouble, then surely (this is the *kal v'chomer*) he is not out of place in making an exception for a human being, whose suffering should not be extended by even one more hour.

[14] The final words in this passage reveal the deep antirabbinic character of this text. Most translations paint the Pharisees discussing various ways of killing Jeshu, "cutting him off from the living." More recent examinations of the Greek word suggest that the plot may be about "cutting him off from teaching." But in either case we see a hostile population of Pharisees that is more consistent with Matthew's biased understanding of Pharisees in his own life-world in the 80s than the actual Pharisees with whom Jeshu dealt in the 20s. This stain of antipharisaism, often spreading over to anti-Judaism, clearly reveals the shadow side of this gospel. In the light of two thousand years of Christian anti-Semitism, these later comments polluting the original teachings of Jeshu seem particularly obscene. It is only by eliminating them that we can disclose the "hidden gospel" that is the goal of our study.

Jeshu went on from there and entered their synagogue, where he encountered a man with a crippled hand. Some people who were looking to find fault with Jeshu[12] asked him whether or not it was permitted to heal on the Sabbath. He responded, "Who among you, if you had just one sheep, would not pull it out of a pit it fell into on a Sabbath? A human being is worth a lot more than a sheep, so of course it's permitted to do good on the Sabbath."[13] Jeshu then said to the man, "Put out your hand." And when he did, it was just as good as the other one. At this point, the Pharisees went out of the synagogue to discuss among themselves how they might cut Jeshu off from teaching.[14] Being aware of what they were plotting, Jeshu left that place.

(*continued on page 101*)

15 Jeshu tells the people he heals not to talk about him. Matthew inherits this from Mark's gospel, and many books have been written about this so-called Marcan secret. Matthew gives us his own perspective on this matter by juxtaposing Jeshu's admonition to secrecy with the quote from Isaiah. Jeshu has been anointed to do God's work; he is indeed a messiah, and he is well aware of that. Nevertheless, his messianic work is not what most of his contemporaries expect. There were messianic claimants preceding Jeshu, and most of them were struggling for the overthrow of Roman rule. Jeshu, however, was a messiah of a different stripe.

16 Second Isaiah consists of chapters 40–55 of the canonical book of Isaiah. These chapters were written after the destruction of Solomon's Temple in 586 B.C.E. At that time, much of the Jewish leadership was taken into exile, and it was there in Babylon that a poet and prophet emerged whose name remains unknown to us and whose oracles now live in a book attributed to another man. This unnamed prophet, whom we now call Second Isaiah, spoke of serving God through vulnerability and vicarious suffering: two themes not prominent in biblical literature before this time.

17 We sense this vulnerability in the words from Isaiah that Matthew uses to preface this healing story. Isaiah's "chosen servant" is loved greatly by God. His mandate is to proclaim justice to all the nations of the world. He will accomplish his mission not through aggressive and argumentative behavior but through sensitivity to others and compassion. Israel saw its own vocational identity in this servant theology, but Matthew understood this material as referring most properly to Jeshu.

Many people followed Jeshu, and he healed all the sick, giving them orders not to talk about him.[15] It was in this way that he fulfilled what is written in the prophet Isaiah:[16] "This is my chosen servant,[17] the one I love and in whom I take delight. I will give him my spirit, and he will proclaim justice to all the nations of the world. He won't argue or shout, nor will his voice be heard in the streets. He'll not break a fragile reed nor quench a flickering wick until justice is completely victorious. All the nations of the world will hope in his name."

(continued on page 103)

18 Without doubt, the exorcising of demons was central to Jeshu's ministry. The background for the story in which the Pharisees confront him regarding the blind and mute demon-possessed man may be Matthew's community rather than the life-world of Jeshu. This is not to say that the kernel of the story may not be from Jeshu's ministry. It is important to note, however, that in either case the controversy is not about the existence of demons or about their being cast out by Jeshu, but rather about any conclusions that can be drawn from this activity. A Jewish tradition develops that sees Jeshu as a magician. Such a development at least acknowledges some evidence of wonder-working, even though it draws different conclusions about its origin.

19 If Satan himself is not made a prisoner, then we had better not presume to cast out the demons who serve him. Jeshu is able to do what he does precisely because he is greater than all the demons and even greater than their chief. His exorcisms, therefore, are evidence that God's reign is actively present in the world. The final choice faced by human beings is whether to support that action or oppose it. To oppose it is to attempt to block the action of God's spirit in the world and thus to be fundamentally off target. There is no neutral territory here. Not to work with Jeshu in his embodiment of the divine activity in the world is to work against him and therefore against God.

20 The question about the unforgivable sin has generated a great deal of scholarly literature. Matthew and Luke are very close on this saying. Only in their common source, Mark, do we find an explanatory verse (Mark 3:30) adding the explanation that some people had accused Jeshu of having an unclean spirit. At one level, we all sin: we all fail in some way, and these sins can be forgiven. In other words, we can readjust our lives and continue on our path. Sinning against God's spirit, however, entails setting ourselves in fundamental opposition to God. Jeshu, however, is so identified with God's spirit that opposition to him translates into blasphemy. This blasphemous enmity toward the way God is acting in the world through Jeshu must be abandoned if one wants to experience God's forgiveness.

Then a demon-possessed man who was both blind and mute was brought to Jeshu, and he healed the man,[18] enabling him once again both to see and speak. The people crowding around them were amazed, asking whether or not Jeshu might be the Son of David. But when the Pharisees heard it, they said: "It's only by Beelzebul, the ruler of the demons, that this man casts out demons." Intuiting their true motives, Jeshu said to them: "Any kingdom filled with internal dissent collapses; and the same thing happens with any city or town. So if we now have Satan driving out Satan, that's a kingdom so filled with internal dissent that it could never survive. Furthermore, if I'm casting out demons with the help of Beelzebul, how are your followers doing it? They will have to be your judges. But if I'm casting out demons with the help of God's spirit, then God's reign is among you."

"How will anyone gain entrance to the house of a strong man and steal his goods without first making the strong man his prisoner?[19] It's only then that he can rob the strong man's house freely. If you're not for me, you're against me; if you're not working with me, you're working against me. By the same token, I want you to know that people can be forgiven all sorts of sins and blasphemies but not a blasphemy against God's spirit. They can even be forgiven speaking against me, but not against the holy spirit.[20] That's something that won't be forgiven, either in this age or in the age that is coming.

(continued on page 105)

21 The teaching about healthy and rotten trees fits this section perfectly. The concern of Jeshu is not with theological orthodoxy but with the way people live in the world. You judge a tree by its fruit, just as you judge institutions and people by the way they act in the world. Religion is something constructed by human beings. It can serve as a vehicle to a good life (and thus be a healthy tree) or it can hinder it (and thus be a rotten tree). The tree will be judged by its fruit. We are not good because we display the right religious labels; we are good when and because we are doing the good that God wants done in our world. This entails two elements of the Buddhists' Eightfold Path: right speech and right action.

22 This passage contains a couple of references to an evil generation. It is not clear whether that phrase comes from Jeshu himself or from the gospel writer. We have already seen Jeshu speaking of his fellow Jews as sheep without a shepherd; now we see them as evil and adulterous. The terms are largely synonymous. To be evil is to be off target somehow, just as we saw that sinning means missing the mark. To be a sheep without a shepherd is similarly to be without proper orientation or direction. Adultery is a common biblical trope for idolatry, pursuing a false god—an ultimate reality other than the one God who covenants with Israel as a lover with the beloved. So adultery, too, in this sense is a lack of proper orientation, not recognizing one's true spouse.

23 When we wander from our center, both the divine center and our own most God-centered self, then we understandably seek our sense of reality outside of ourselves. This is why the people in this text ask for a sign. The irony, of course, is that they are asking for a sign in the face of the one who is par excellence the sign of God's presence and activity in the world. Jonah was a sign in the past, as was Solomon, and now someone greater than Jonah or Solomon is among them, though the people lack receptivity to both messenger and message.

"Either come up with a healthy tree and healthy fruit or a rotten tree and rotten fruit, for we judge trees by their fruit.[21] How can you expect to say good things when you're basically evil, like a pit of snakes? Our lips express what's building up in our hearts. Good people come out with good things because they're filled with what is good; bad people come out with bad things because they're filled with what is bad. I want you to know that on judgment day you'll be held responsible for all the ways you've misused your power of speech. For your words will show you to be either God-centered or God-damned."

At this point some of the Torah scholars and Pharisees said to Jeshu, "Teacher, we'd like a sign from you." Jeshu answered them: "This is an evil and adulterous generation[22] that is seeking a sign, and the only sign it's getting is the sign of the prophet Jonah.[23] For just as Jonah was in the belly of the monster for three days and three nights, so too will I be in the heart of the earth for three days and three nights. At the judgment, the people of Nineveh will stand up and condemn this generation, for when the Ninevites heard Jonah preach, they turned their lives around. Are you aware that someone greater than Jonah is here with you now? At the judgment, the queen of the south will stand up and condemn this generation, for she came from the ends of the earth to listen to Solomon's wisdom. Are you aware that someone greater than Solomon is here with you now?

(continued on page 107)

24 The teaching about the unclean spirits and their residence in human beings follows nicely. It does not help a person to have a demon exorcised if the Divine Spirit fails to make its abode in that person's heart. If a vacuum remains at the heart's center, something will fill it, and more than likely it will be the same evil spirit returning, though now with seven companions even worse than itself. It is not only nature that abhors a vacuum; so too does the spiritual life.

We do not ordinarily obtain a cup of coffee by first using a complicated mechanism to vacuum out the air from the cup; we simply pour in the coffee and displace the air. So too we do not get rid of our neuroses and bad habits only to find ourselves left with an empty house. Such a house calls back the expelled spirits. If, on the other hand, we are open to healthy and holy influences, the evil spirits will be expelled and their places will be filled by the forces of good.

25 We notice the absence of Jeshu's father, Josef, from this family visit—a detail suggesting that he is dead by the time of Jeshu's public ministry. Like any group in which we are socialized, a family structure can function as a grid blocking our perception of reality. It can be part of that habitual way of seeing the world that has to be broken in order to accomplish the *metanoia,* the change of mind, to which the gospel challenges us. Jeshu may have seen this as particularly true because of the strongly patriarchal character of the family structure in his lifeworld, especially if he was proposing a model of table fellowship in which we are all brothers and sisters, children of the same heavenly Parent. Jeshu's calling people to discipleship undoubtedly ruptured some family groupings and challenged some family expectations.

"When an unclean spirit leaves a person, it wanders through desert places looking for rest. Finding none, it decides to go back to the house it left, and there everything stands vacant, clean, and in order.[24] The unclean spirit then goes out and finds seven other spirits worse than itself, and they take up their residence in that poor soul. In this way, the person is worse off at the end than he was before. And that's exactly what will happen to this evil generation."

While Jeshu was still talking to the crowds, his mother and brothers happened to be outside, and someone told Jeshu that they wanted to speak with him. Jeshu answered, "Who is my mother and who are my brothers?" Then pointing to his disciples, Jeshu said, "Look at these disciples of mine; they are my mother and my brothers.[25] For whoever does the will of my heavenly Parent is my brother, my sister, and my mother too."

△ Parables are Jeshu's favorite form of teaching. Someone has remarked that parables are characterized by shortness, sense, and salt. Like a good joke, a parable has a punch line. A student of mine commented once that when a parable really works for you, it is much like falling out of bed. It creates in the listener that "aha!" reaction, the breakthrough of insight that sometimes finds expression in a great laugh. The best effect comes from hearing these parables for the first time. Many Christians are jaded from the frequent repetition of them in Sunday services. If we are not hearing them for the first time, at least we can hear them with fresh ears.

1 The parable of the sower contains one of the most fundamental spiritual teachings to be found in any of the great sacred traditions. The allegorical explanation that follows (the part that begins with Jeshu's offering to explain the parable) comes from the catechetical teachings of the early community of Christians, and it is not as relevant for our purposes. After all, if it was a good parable to begin with, Jeshu should not have to explain it. Furthermore, any explanation pins down the deliberate ambiguity of the story in which its very genius lies.

2 What strikes us in this story? In one sense, explaining a parable is a bit like explaining a joke. The more we have to talk about it, the less funny (and pointed) it is. But it seems that one thing that might break through for us as we hear the words is that the seed is perfectly adequate in every case. The different degrees of productivity have nothing to do with any difference in the seed. It is the quality of the receiving element that is at issue. One can be an unprotected path, rocky ground, shallow soil, soil already rife with thorny weeds, or receptive soil. In the last analysis, the parable is all about the soil.

6 □ Teaching in Parables
(Matthew 13:1-58)

Jeshu left the house that same day and went to teach down by the sea-side. So many people came crowding around him that he climbed into a boat and sat down there to teach while the crowds stood on the shore. He told them many things that day, speaking to them in parables.[1]

"Pay attention. One day a fellow went out to sow some seed.[2] As he sowed, some seed fell on the path, and birds came and ate it. Other seed fell on rocky ground, where there wasn't much soil. The seeds sprouted quickly, since the soil wasn't deep; but when the sun came up, the little plants withered quickly, too, since they had no roots. Other seed fell among thorny bushes that climbed up and choked the young plants. Still other seed fell on fertile soil and produced grain—in some cases, a full 100 percent sprouted; otherwise, 60 percent or 30 percent. If you open your ears, you can understand this."

At this point his disciples asked Jeshu why he was speaking in these parables, and he replied, "I'm speaking this way because you are being given knowledge of the mysteries of God's reign, but this is not being given to these others. For the one who is rich will receive even more and will enjoy abundance, but the one who is poor will lose even the little he has. If I talk to these people in parables, it's because even with their eyes open they don't see, and even with their ears open they neither hear nor understand.

(continued on page 111)

3 The discussion between Jeshu and his disciples after his delivery of the parable of the sower seems open to misinterpretation. Perhaps the confusion is already somehow present in the text as we have it. The quotation from Isaiah does not necessarily help clarify the issue. It is possible to read this whole exchange in such a way that one goes away with the impression that Jeshu was teaching in parables in order to confuse people. In other words, he wanted people not to understand him, and he would give the clear meaning to his disciples offstage later.

Such an interpretation would be an absurd inversion of any teaching vocation and certainly of a compassionate ministry such as that of Jeshu. No spiritual teacher would purposely try to be misunderstood. Nevertheless, misunderstanding does indeed plague the teacher of spiritual wisdom. One has only to recall how the Buddha, after his initial enlightenment, fought off many temptations but was nearly unsettled by one final temptation suggesting that he would teach for some forty-five years and not find even one listener who would understand him. The Buddha responded that despite the obvious truth that many would miss the point, some would indeed understand and assimilate his message, and that was enough. It was only after overcoming this final temptation that he could walk to the nearby park to deliver his first sermon.

⚶ Spiritual teachings can be like strong spring rains that damage delicately petaled buds while nourishing great oaks. The very strength of a teaching's truth can crush one hearer of the word while strengthening another. Would it really make sense to tell the average ten-year-old child that human life means learning how to die, how to let go of all clinging and cultivate the readiness to lose absolutely everything? And yet, a spiritually mature person can find great comfort, inspiration, and strength in that same teaching. Jeshu's teachings will be misunderstood far more than understood, and they will even be misunderstood by his disciples, and later by those who bear his name.

⚶ It is very human for us to want to hide from ourselves, to develop layers of protective neuroses so that we will not see or hear our own

(continued on page 112)

"You can experience in them the fulfillment of Isaiah's prophetic oracle: 'You will listen and listen, but not understand; you will look and look, but not see. For this people's heart is dull and their ears are blocked and their eyes are closed, because they don't want to see with their eyes or hear with their ears. For then their hearts would understand, they would turn their lives around, and I would heal them.'³

"It's a blessing that you have eyes that see and ears that hear. You can believe me when I tell you that many prophets and God-centered people wanted with all their hearts to see what you see but didn't, wanted with all their hearts to hear what you hear but didn't.

"Let me explain to you the parable of the fellow sowing seed. Those who hear the word of God's reign and don't understand it are like the seed that fell on the path; they are pounced on by the Evil One, who snatches away what was sown in their hearts. Those who receive the word enthusiastically as soon as they hear it are like the seed that fell on rocky ground. Having no roots, they have a short-lived faith; when trial or persecution come along because of the word they received, they soon disappear. Those who hear the word but then find that worldly concerns and their preoccupation with making money choke out everything else are like the seed that fell near the thorny bushes, where no grain ever appeared. But those who hear the word, understand it, and produce grain at a rate of 100 percent, 60 percent, or 30 percent are like the seed that fell on fertile ground."

(continued on page 113)

reality. A culture of denial and distraction like ours makes this even easier for us to do. Most of Jeshu's hearers wanted to be amused, to be entertained by signs, and to be titillated with clever anecdotes, but they did not really want to be healed. I know a man who has gone to a therapist for years but who told me once that he has never shared with his therapist what really bothers him. Spiritual truths can blind us like floodlights or burn us like lasers; they can also illuminate us and heal us.

4 We find a trinity of parables here: wheat and weeds, mustard seed, and yeast. The parable of wheat and weeds is often read in an eschatological mode. Saints and sinners live together in the world, but when the final trumpet is blown, heaven receives the former while the latter dissolve into the flames of hell. There is, of course, another way of understanding this. Everything human is mixed; monasteries and brothels house both saints and sinners. There is neither a "righteous coalition" nor an "axis of evil." Weeds and wheat grow together everywhere—in every church, in every country, and in every human heart. It is only from the perspective of God's reign that we can properly discern the mingled patchwork that is both within and outside of us.

5 In a world that worships size—we are hardly different from the ancient Roman Empire in that regard—the small seems inconsequential. The twin parables about the mustard seed and the yeast contain the same awakening insight, a dramatic reversal of that whole presupposition. For who had not seen that smallest seed, something with which any peasant in Jeshu's life-world would be familiar, grow into a huge bush? Even the birds are convinced that it is large enough to be a secure place for their nesting. And yet, what a small beginning. Does not the pinch of yeast explode with much the same meaning? Often as a child in my grandmother's kitchen I lifted the towel laid over the large mixing bowl and marveled at the dough rising within it. How could that bit of yeast produce such a miraculous change?

6 These two parables fairly ripple with meaning. A spiritual truth, like a tiny seed or a pinch of yeast, can transform a life, and then a community,

(continued on page 114)

Jeshu told them another parable: "God's reign is like a farmer who sowed good seed on his land. His enemy came one night when everyone was asleep, sowed weeds in his wheat fields, and sneaked away.[4] The result was that when the wheat began to grow, so too did the weeds. His farmworkers came to him wondering why there were so many weeds when only good seed had been sown on the land. The farmer told them that an enemy had done this. 'Do you want us to try to pick all the weeds?' asked the farmworkers. 'No,' answered the farmer, 'we don't want to risk harming the wheat. Let them grow together until harvest time; then I will have the reapers gather the weeds first and tie them up in bundles for burning; after that, they can bring the wheat into my barn.'"

Jeshu told them another parable: "God's reign is like a mustard seed[5] that a farmer took and planted in his field. It's a very small seed, but when the plant appears, it's such a large bush that it actually appears to be a tree. Birds even fly down to make nests in its branches." Jeshu told them another parable: "God's reign is like a pinch of yeast that a woman takes and mixes with a large bowl of flour until the whole batch of dough rises."

Jeshu spoke to the crowds only in parables, telling them nothing except in the form of parables. By doing this he fulfilled the prophetic oracle that says: "I will open my mouth in parables and reveal things hidden from the beginning."

(continued on page 115)

and then a world. Jeshu's teachings are both seeds and yeast. So too is Jeshu himself—a peasant who probably never wandered more than sixty miles in any one direction (I regard the flight to and return from Egypt as Matthew's midrash) and certainly sent no written letters or books to the four corners of the earth—and yet the world blossoms with his teachings, and millions eat of his bread. And is Matthew's little band not such a seed and such a bit of yeast as well?

6 These parables of Jeshu enter our language and life with remarkable ease. He was indeed a master of metaphor. The treasure, the pearl, and the fish all make the same point. What is it that stands above everything else in our lives? To use Paul Tillich's apt phrase, what is our ultimate concern? How we answer that question can lay bare our entire life in all its manifold complexity.

For Jeshu, the answer to this question is clear: God and God's reign. As Rabbi Heschel once remarked, God is either of supreme importance or of no importance. "God's reign" refers to our own consciousness of that divine reality, our assimilation of that mystery, and its incorporation into our life choices. Discernment is needed in these choices—to identify a real treasure, an exceptional pearl, or a wonderful fish. If our answer to the question about what stands above everything else in our lives points to something unable to bear the weight of ultimacy, then we are choosing a lifetime of disappointment and frustration. We have then invested something with ultimacy that is unable to fulfill that promise.

& Unfortunately, an editor's hand has sent the wonderful parable of the fish in a totally different direction. This is where we see the necessity of discovering the "hidden gospel" underlying the received text. Matthew's community is preoccupied with a coming apocalyptic judgment, and Jeshu's teachings provide grist for his mill. Instead of stressing the joy of the man who pulls out the great fish that will provide a wonderful dinner for his family, the author distracts our focus to the process of separating good fish from bad. This leads Matthew to paint an end-time scenario in which all who clone his faith are rewarded

(continued on page 116)

Then Jeshu sent the multitudes away and went back into the house. Following him inside, his disciples asked him to explain to them the parable of the weeds in the farmer's field. Jeshu answered them: "I am the one who sows the good seed in the field. And the field stands for the world itself, just as the good seed refers to the children of God's reign. The weeds, on the other hand, are the children of the Evil One, for the one who sowed them is none other than the Devil. The harvest is the end of the age, and the reapers are angels. Just as the weeds are bundled up and thrown into the fire, so will it be at the end of the age. I will send my angels to gather up all those who hindered God's reign by acting apart from the teachings of the Torah. The angels will throw these people into the fire, where they will weep and grind their teeth in despair. Then at last the God-centered people will shine out, bright as the sun, in the sky of God's reign. If you open your ears, you can understand this.

"God's reign is like a treasure hidden in a field. Someone finds the treasure by chance and covers it up again. Out of sheer joy, this person then runs off to sell everything he has so that he can come up with the money to buy the field. Another image of God's reign is that of a businessman who is in the market for pearls. When he finds one that is exceptionally valuable, he heads off to sell everything he has to buy that pearl.[6]

"You could also say that God's reign is like a net thrown out into the sea—a net that is soon teeming with all kinds of fish. The fishermen draw it in when it's full and then sit down on the shore and divide the fish, putting the good fish in buckets and throwing back the worthless ones. This is how it will be at the end of the age. The angels will go out and divide the wicked from the God-centered. They will throw the wicked into a furnace of fire, where they will weep and grind their teeth in despair."

(*continued on page 117*)

and those who differ from him are damned—a sad decline from the level at which Jeshu was teaching.

7 The telling image of the homeowner who goes into his storage room, bringing out treasures both old and new, may well be a code word for the unknown final editor and author of this gospel. He knows how to weave together the personages, stories, and promises of the Hebrew Bible with the new teachings of the man from the Galilee, the suffering Messiah whom God raised from the dead, the teacher of a new Torah, the child of Abraham and of David, the new Moses and the new Jeremiah, the one who would come again as eschatological judge of all of human history. Every interpreter, translator, and commentator repeats and renews this process.

8 Mark's gospel calls Jeshu a carpenter; Matthew refers to him only as the carpenter's son. Although we cannot presume that we have recorded dialogue here, it is nonetheless interesting that the context of the remark attributed to his townspeople might suggest that Jeshu had been away for a while. Is there some uncertainty about who this hometown boy is who has just walked into the synagogue? Might we conclude that he has been absent for a period of time? And, if so, where has he been? This question has generated numerous answers accounting for these so-called lost years. He was in Egypt learning magic. He visited India where he studied with some of the great yogis. He was in Qumran with the Essenes.

9 Whatever accounts for his absence, Jeshu appears in his hometown synagogue after some years away and finds himself less than hospitably greeted by his former neighbors. The criticisms of his larger society have followed him home. Matthew omits the even more hostile reaction described by Mark, including the embarrassing comment that his relatives thought they should put him away as someone insane (Mark 3:21). Matthew also softens Mark's comment that he could perform *no* miracles there, indicating instead that he could not perform "*many* powerful deeds there."

Jeshu then asked his disciples if they understood all these teachings, and they assured him that they did. He then said to them, "Every Torah scholar, then, who becomes a disciple of God's reign is like a rich home-owner who goes into his storage room and brings out both old and new treasures."[7]

When Jeshu finished teaching all these parables, he left that place and went back to his old neighborhood. He taught in their synagogue, and those who heard him asked in amazement, "Where did he come up with this wisdom and this power? Isn't this the carpenter's son,[8] whose mother is called Miriam and whose brothers are Jacob, Joseph, Shimon, and Judah? Don't all his sisters live right here in the neighborhood?" They were clearly very upset by Jeshu's presence, and he said to them, "Where else but in his own neighborhood and in his own house would a prophet go without recognition?" And because of their lack of trust, Jeshu didn't perform many powerful deeds there.[9]

1 We find the story of Jochanan's execution in the writings of the Jewish historian Josephus, although there we find no account of the dance and the promise. But the twirling veils, the lithe and lovely dancer, the lusty king, the devious queen, and the grisly execution have all become part of our cultural heritage. Herod's remark reflects the casual acceptance of a bizarre mixture of resurrection and reincarnation. Or is he merely saying that the spirit of Jochanan now lives in this Jeshu? What is most important in this narrative is, first, that Herod now knows about Jeshu and, second, that he understands and interprets him as a clone of his predecessor and mentor, the very same Jochanan whom he has executed. And that, of course, does not bode well for Jeshu's safety. According to Matthew's midrash, it was Herod Antipas's father, Herod the Great, who had tried but failed to eliminate Jeshu when he was but a baby. Might the son achieve what his father failed to accomplish?

2 We can only imagine what Jeshu mused about during his attempted retreat in one of the fishing boats. Certainly he feels a sense of loss for a friend and mentor. He might also feel some fear regarding the implied danger to himself as one of Jochanan's followers. In the atmosphere of paranoia inevitably produced by tyranny, Jeshu surely realizes that any Jew attracting a following will be held suspect by the reigning powers, for it was the consistent policy of Rome to ruthlessly eliminate potential messiahs and their suspect followers.

7 □ A Mentor's Death Brings New Challenges (Matthew 14:1-16:12)

Word of Jeshu reached King Herod Antipas at this time, and he said to his courtiers, "This Jeshu must be Jochanan the Immerser raised from the dead; that would explain all the power that is being manifested in him." Now this is the same Herod who had ordered Jochanan's arrest and imprisonment. Herod had done this because of his own involvement with Herodias, the wife of his brother Philip. For Jochanan had told Herod that it was immoral for him to take Herodias as his wife.

Herod, of course, wanted to have Jochanan killed immediately, but he was afraid of the masses of people who considered Jochanan a prophet. But when Herod's birthday came around, the daughter of Herodias danced in front of the whole court. Herod was so entranced by this display that he promised under oath to give her whatever she wanted. Taking her cue from her mother, the girl requested the head of Jochanan the Immerser on a serving dish. The king was upset by this request, but, because of the oath he had taken in front of all his guests, he saw no other choice but to give orders that her wish be granted. The result was that he sent some of his men to behead Jochanan in prison.[1] The head was brought to the girl on a serving dish, and she gave it to her mother. The disciples of Jochanan then came to take the body and bury it, and they're the ones who then brought word of all this to Jeshu.

When Jeshu heard this news, he took a boat and headed off by himself to a deserted area.[2]

(continued on page 121)

3 Jeshu's planned retreat fails to materialize. The crowds are waiting for him: people oppressed by foreign occupation, poverty, disease, and hunger. Once again, Jeshu puts aside his own needs because of his feeling for these people and their problems. He provides healing and food, the two things they most desperately need. I am reminded here of the insightful words of Oscar Wilde: "He [Jesus] understood the leprosy of the leper, the darkness of the blind, the fierce misery of those who live for pleasure, the strange poverty of the rich." Jeshu was truly a man for others.

4 Stories of miraculous multiplication of food occur in all four of the canonical gospels. I do not dispute the point that an adept like Jeshu had unusual powers and could, if he desired, multiply food. My concern lies in the fact that adepts are generally reluctant to use these *siddhis* (paranormal powers). Highly evolved souls tend to be aware of the danger of these powers, both for themselves and for the people who see their use. The former can be tempted to spiritual narcissism; the latter can be turned into spectators of, instead of participants in, the divine drama.

Perhaps this story of the multiplication of loaves and fishes can best be interpreted more as a learning moment than a magic show. Only a small amount of food seems to be available. But when Jeshu blesses it and begins to pass it around, others are led to share what little they have stashed away to stave off hunger. A piece of cheese here, a crust of bread there, some grapes, a few figs. People begin to take out whatever they had been hoarding and pass it around. And in the end everyone is satisfied. With a hyperbolic flourish, the narrator mentions leftovers.

If Jeshu had simply opted to multiply food, what would people have learned? They would have felt less self-reliant, and perhaps they even would have felt some resentment that this magician chose to feed them on this particular day while letting them go hungry on so many others. What he did, instead, was give them an example of how even poor people can take care of one another—a lesson they could take home with them, more important even than the food in their bellies.

But as soon as the crowds got wind of this, they poured out of the town and went around the lake by foot to get to the place where his boat was heading. When Jeshu stepped ashore, he saw a large crowd of people waiting for him.[3] Feeling deep compassion for them, he healed all their sick.

As it grew dark, his disciples came to him and said, "This is a lonely place, and the daylight is just about gone. Why don't you send the crowds away now so that they can go to some of the villages around here to get something to eat?" "They don't need to go away," said Jeshu. "You can give them something to eat." "But we don't have anything here except five loaves of bread and two fish," they answered. "Have the crowd come over here," said Jeshu. With that, he asked the crowd to sit down on the grass. Then he took the five loaves of bread and the two fish, and, raising his eyes heavenward, he said the blessing, broke the bread, and gave it to his disciples, who in turn shared it with the crowd. Everyone ate as much as they wanted, and it still took twelve baskets to hold all the leftover bread. All in all, about five thousand men ate that day, not counting the women and children.[4]

(continued on page 123)

5 As with the multiplication of food, I find it credible that Jeshu, like other spiritual adepts, could indeed walk on water, but I am not sure that he would. I wonder if this is more a parable of faith? Matthew's community must often have felt like a little boat tossed about on a stormy sea, buffeted by the polemics of the rabbinic leadership and threatened by the cruelty of the Roman authorities. They wanted to reach Jeshu through their faith, their trust, but they often found themselves sinking in the turbulent waters that engulfed them. Shimon, the so-called Rock, represented every one of these early Jeshu followers. And it was Jeshu alone, the Lord of their community, who could cause these waters to subside and bring them home to the shores of security and peace.

⚠ It seems to me that we need constantly to remind ourselves that this gospel was not written as a documentary account of factual data. Gospels are portraits of faith. Their purpose is to propel the reader into a process through which life is creatively transformed. Jeshu is not simply a fact of history for them but the living Lord of their community, their dynamic link with the divine mystery and its purposes in the world. As they recall the stories passed on about Jeshu, these stories take on the texture of faith; they carry a significance that transcends their literal meaning. This is not fabrication, much less prevarication, but parable, midrash, and testimony to spiritual experience. To read these stories through the lenses of literalism is to miss the point.

6 The Pharisees' challenge to Jeshu fits his life-world. They defined certain traditions as essential to their idea of table fellowship, and they could well be chiding Jeshu and his *chavura* for being negligent in these matters. It is, of course, equally possible to see this altercation set in the life-world of Matthew's community, where rabbinic Jews and Christians brandished competing halachas (legal codes). The distinction between human tradition and divine command forms an ongoing matrix for religious conversation. What Christian does not know a case of the faithful parishioner who volunteers for every church function and sings

(continued on page 124)

After this, Jeshu asked his disciples to get into the boat and meet him on the other side of the lake while he stayed behind to send home the crowd of people. When he had finished sending them home, Jeshu went up by himself into the nearby hills to pray. As the day turned to evening he was still there alone. Meanwhile, the boat filled with his disciples was at that very moment being tossed about by high waves and hostile winds in the middle of the lake. It was just before dawn when Jeshu came to them, walking on the surface of the lake.[5]

Seeing Jeshu walking on the water, the disciples were terrified. They cried out in fear that they must be seeing a ghost. But he immediately said to them, "Hang on; it's me; don't be afraid!" At this point, Rock said to Jeshu, "If it's really you, Lord, call me to come to you on the water." "Come on, then," Jeshu said to him. So Rock climbed out of the boat and started walking toward Jeshu on the water. Noticing the wind whipping around him, Rock began to be afraid, and, starting to sink, he cried out to Jeshu, "Lord, save me!" Jeshu immediately reached out his hand and caught him, saying to him, "How little trust you have. Why did you doubt?"

When Jeshu and Rock climbed aboard, the winds immediately dropped. Then the disciples in the boat were all at Jeshu's feet, saying to him, "You really are God's son."

When they finished crossing the lake, they landed at Genesar. Some of the men in that area recognized Jeshu and got the word out to all the people nearby, who brought their sick to him. They begged Jeshu to let the sick just touch his *tzitzit*, and as many as did so were healed.

After this, Jeshu was approached by some Pharisees and Torah scholars from Jerusalem, who asked him, "Why are your disciples unobservant of the tradition of the elders by not washing their hands before they break bread together?"[6]

(continued on page 125)

lustily in the choir, but at the same time her children go neglected, seeking in vain for some quality time with their absentee parent? How often God's will is violated in the name of the religious traditions we ourselves have created.

7 The whole issue of inner and outer cleanliness is crucial. Mark 7:18–20 seems to suggest that Jeshu is abolishing the food laws completely. That, however, makes no sense at all, since the question will later be hotly debated in the early church, and it takes a special vision to Shimon (Acts 10:9–16) to convince him that he is no longer bound by kashrut, the dietary laws. If Jeshu had settled the matter so unambiguously, such drastic measures would not be needed. Since Matthew's community probably observed the food laws, he changed the text of Mark to make certain in his gospel that Jeshu's words are not misunderstood. His editing in this case may take us closer to Jeshu's original teaching on this matter.

🔯 If Jeshu was not abolishing the dietary laws, what was he doing? Jeshu was a teacher of *kavanah,* of intentionality and inwardness. He did not deny *keva,* the regular observances of Jewish life. But he did continually challenge *keva,* trying to make sure that it never displaced the deeper principles in which all authentic practice is rooted. Dietary laws and other practices surrounding the eating of food can have their place, as long as they are understood as subordinate to the more important issues that define and identify truly religious people. A friend of mine is a Buddhist priest and a vegetarian, and yet he makes it a point to eat whatever is served by his host when he is dining out. Being considerate as a guest ranks higher for him than maintaining his dietary purity.

In response, Jeshu said to them, "And why is it that because of your tradition you are unobservant of the commandment of God? For God commanded us to honor our parents and further said that those who curse their parents are worthy of death. But you claim that those who make an offering to God of monies that are needed to help their parents are in no way dishonoring them. And yet this tradition of yours denies God's word. You mock true observance in doing this, and you fit the words that Isaiah spoke in prophecy when he said: 'This people pays me lip service, but they hold their hearts far from me; their religion is ridiculous, because what they are teaching are human inventions.'"

Then Jeshu gathered a crowd of people around him and said, "I want you to hear and understand what I'm saying. It's not what goes into our mouths that can make us unclean but what comes out of our mouths."[7] At this point his disciples came up to him and said, "Do you realize that the Pharisees are really upset in hearing this teaching?" But Jeshu merely said, "Every plant not planted by my heavenly Parent is going to be uprooted. Don't worry about those Pharisees. They're blind leaders, and when one blind person leads another person equally blind, they both end up falling in the ditch." Rock spoke up at this point and asked Jeshu to explain this parable. Jeshu asked, "Are you missing the point just as much as they are? Don't you understand that whatever goes into our mouths passes through our intestines and is then eliminated? But the things that come out of our mouths come from our hearts, and those are the things that can make us unclean. For it's in the heart that evil thoughts originate, along with murder, sexual immorality, theft, lies about other people, and false oaths made in God's name. These are what make people unclean. But to omit washing one's hands before breaking bread—no one becomes unclean that way!"

(continued on page 127)

8 This exchange with the Gentile woman is a difficult piece of tradition. It may have been added by Matthew, but there seems to be no compelling reason for him to do so. Presuming, then, that this dialogue stems from Jeshu himself, can we make sense of it? Jeshu, for a reason not stated in the text, has crossed the historical borders of Israel and is in foreign territory. He apparently has no awareness of a call to reach out beyond the borders of his Jewish world. We have seen him respond to Romans, but they at least live within the borders of his country, albeit in the most intrusive form possible—as a foreign occupying force. This woman, on the other hand, lives outside those borders and is someone with whom he should have no relationship, indeed no interest in whatsoever.

In the narrative itself, Jeshu ignores the woman and addresses her only after the importunities of his disciples. Her request surprises him and challenges him. He responds with a remark that is disturbingly tribal; it includes the identification of the non-Jew as a dog, a common derogatory term in less inclusive Jewish circles. We might expect the exchange to end with this rebuff, but the woman accepts the insulting implication of Jeshu's comment, thus turning it into a clever riposte. Jeshu seems thoroughly Middle Eastern in his enjoyment of this gutsy response, and he (perhaps laughingly) capitulates to it.

9 Jeshu sits on one of the hills along the lake where he is most at home. He reaches out in healing to all who are brought to him. The Galilee was a region of mixed populations, and there is no reason to presume that everyone coming to him that day was Jewish. But this no longer matters. His heavenly Parent's love and healing extend to everyone. Jeshu's own ego seems totally to disappear at this point, because the people are no longer inclined to attach praise to him. They seem to recognize finally that he is indeed only a vehicle of the divine mystery, and so it is that they praise not him but the God he worships, serves, and proclaims. This God of Israel does not belong to Israel alone; this God belongs to the world, as does this servant of God.

Leaving that area, Jeshu proceeded to the district of Tyre and Sidon. A Phoenician woman from those parts came to him, crying out, "Show compassion to me, Lord, Son of David; my daughter is cruelly tormented by a demon." But Jeshu didn't say a word to her. His disciples came up to him and said, "Get rid of her! She's following after us and making a commotion." Jeshu replied, "I haven't been sent for anyone but the lost sheep of the House of Israel." But the woman nevertheless approached Jeshu and, falling at his feet, said, "Lord, help me." Jeshu responded, "But it's not a good idea to take the children's food and give it to the dogs." "That's true, Lord," she replied, "but even the dogs eat the scraps that fall from the tables of their masters." "You are quite a woman," Jeshu said "and you have shown an extraordinary degree of trust; everything will turn out just as you want." Her daughter was healed precisely at that time.[8]

Leaving that region, Jeshu went along the shore of Lake Kinneret. Going up into the hills, he sat down there. Large crowds came to him, bringing with them those who were lame, blind, crippled, and mute, along with many other kinds of sick people. They put them down at Jeshu's feet, and he healed them. The crowds were amazed when they saw mute people speaking, crippled people cured, lame people walking, and blind people seeing. One and all, they praised the God of Israel.[9]

(continued on page 129)

[10] This is largely a repetition of the earlier multiplication story, with only a difference in details. In both multiplication stories we note that Jeshu says the blessing. The blessing can also be understood as a thanksgiving. The traditional blessing contains a reference to the transcendent God followed by a connection to the action at hand. In the blessing of the bread, for example, one has the traditional beginning: "Blessed are You, O Lord God, King of the Universe," followed by "Who causes bread to come forth from the earth." Understanding Jeshu's own spirituality entails paying attention to these blessings, which run like a string of pearls through the actions of his day. These blessings are ways of giving thanks in every miracle moment.

[⚛] This spirituality is one of blessed participation. It is by taking part in earthly life in all its richness that we encounter the divine mystery. As Martin Buber reminds us, the world is not an obstacle on the way to God; it is the way. This message is reinforced by a passage in the Palestinian Talmud admonishing us that we will be called into account on the last day for all the joys of creation in which we failed to participate. We bless God as we drink wine, eat bread, see a wonder of creation, marvel at children, enjoy making love with our partners, and drink deeply of each day's fullness.

[11] Pharisees and Sadducees coming to put Jeshu to the test about signs might reflect an authentic interchange, although Pharisees and Sadducees (traditional enemies) acting together seems less than likely. The comments about reading the signs of the weather seem consonant with Jeshu's teaching style and the rural tenor of many of his images. It would also make sense, in the light of his teaching about the availability of God's reign, that he would talk about reading the signs of spiritual opportunities. That is, after all, his primary message. Heaven's gates are open to all of us in every moment; we have only to be receptive to the larger life that constitutes our rightful legacy. That entails letting go of the ego agenda to which we cling so persistently.

At this point, Jeshu called his disciples over and said to them, "I'm really worried about these people; they've been with me three days now without having anything to eat. I don't want to send them away hungry, because they might not make it home." The disciples said to him, "But where can we find enough food in this deserted place to feed a crowd like this?" Jeshu asked them, "How many loaves of bread do you have with you?" They told him that they had seven loaves of bread and a few fish. Jeshu invited the crowd to sit down on the ground. Then he took the seven loaves of bread and the fish, and, after saying the blessing, he broke the bread and gave it to his disciples, who distributed it to the crowds. And when they had all eaten as much as they wanted, they collected seven baskets of leftovers. Some four thousand men had eaten, not counting the women and children.[10] Sending the crowds away, Jeshu got into the boat and went to the hilly region around Magdala.

Some Pharisees and Sadducees came to Jeshu to put him to the test,[11] asking him to show them some heavenly sign.

(continued on page 131)

12 The reference to the sign of Jonah probably comes from the community, since it clearly refers to the resurrection. Just as Jonah emerged from the belly of the fish after three days (Jonah 1:17), so does Jeshu emerge from the tomb three days after his death. Since there is no evidence that physical resurrection occurred, there is little likelihood that Jeshu ever talked about it. What we are seeing here are the concerns of the community gathered in his name some fifty years after his death. The narrative traces the gradual shift from the existentially challenging teaching of Jeshu about the availability of God's reign to the imminence of the *parousia,* his glorious return.

Such an emendation of Jeshu's teaching is understandable, though unfortunate. Understandable, because we humans always prefer doing almost anything over being in the moment with the full weight of its challenge. Unfortunate, because this becomes part of the tragic trajectory whereby Christian spirituality became increasingly less open to God's presence and availability in the moment and more exercised about the day and hour of Jeshu's return.

Just as a physical resurrection is misunderstood midrash, so too is any hope for a physical return of Jeshu on the clouds. The *parousia,* or glorious return of Jeshu, points to the evolution of humankind to a more mystical mode of existence. The return of Jeshu, in other words, is a metaphor for the movement of humankind into the "Christ consciousness" or the "Buddha consciousness" or whatever name we want to give to a heightened contact with spiritual reality. In all of these personal and societal transformations, Jeshu returns in glory.

13 The discussion of yeast seems to reflect the community's agenda more than anything relating to the ministry of the historical Jeshu. Yeast was used in a positive sense in the parable Jeshu told about the small amount of yeast raising the great lump of dough. Yeast in a negative sense is more consistent with the Jewish usage of the time. The coupling of the normal usage with the critique of the pharisaic teachings locates this episode in the life-world of the community.

But he answered them by saying, "A red sky at sunset is a sign of fair weather for you, just as a red and overcast sky in the morning tells you that stormy weather is coming. Since you know how to read these signs so well, why can't you discern the signs of spiritual opportunities? People always looking for signs are missing the mark and chasing after idols. No sign will be given to them except the sign of Jonah."[12] And with that answer, he left them and walked away.

The disciples, in crossing to the other side of the lake, had forgotten to bring along any food. Jeshu said to them, "Watch out and be on your guard for the yeast of the Pharisees and Sadducees." The disciples, in talking among themselves, presumed that he was referring to the fact that they had forgotten to bring along any food. Realizing this, Jeshu said to them, "Why are you talking about food? You are people with such little trust. Do you still not understand? Have you forgotten the five thousand people, the five loaves of bread, and how many baskets of leftovers you filled? Or what about the four thousand people, the seven loaves of bread, and all the containers of leftovers you filled? How can you think that I was talking to you about food when I told you to watch out for the yeast[13] of the Pharisees and Sadducees." And so they finally understood that he wasn't telling them to watch out for the literal yeast of the Pharisees and Sadducees but to watch out for their teachings.

1 The discussion of how people are identifying Jeshu presumes ideas of reincarnation. Otherwise, how can Jeshu possibly be Jeremiah, who died centuries before Jeshu was born? This indicates the prevalence of reincarnational thinking in the Jewish world at this time. Jewish mysticism continues to teach *gilgul ha nefesh,* the doctrine of reincarnation, and many of the hasidic leaders were recognized as reincarnations of former rabbis and sages. So asking if Jeshu might be Jeremiah is not foreign to the thought world of first-century Judaism. The case with Elijah is slightly different, since the biblical text indicates that he had never died.

2 One function of this gospel was certainly to provide catechesis, or instruction for new members of the community. Understood that way, we can see why Jeshu is first introduced in his active life as teacher, healer, and exorcist. Exposure to Jeshu is expected to lead the catechumen to acknowledge that Jeshu is indeed the Christ, God's anointed one, the Messiah. Then the initiate is introduced to the second level of teaching, everything involving suffering and death, all that we associate with Jeshu's passion. This is why Rock's confession of faith in Jeshu as Messiah is considered the centerpiece and turning point of this entire gospel.

8 ☐ Who Is This Man?
(Matthew 16:13-18:35)

When Jeshu came into the neighborhood of Caesarea Philippi, he asked his disciples, "Who do people say that I am?" "Some say you're Jochanan the Immerser," they answered, "but others say you're Elijah or Jeremiah or some other prophet."**1** "But what about you," he said to them; "who do you say that I am?" Shimon Rock said in response, "You're the Messiah, the son of the living God."**2** "God bless you for saying that, Shimon, son of Jonah," answered Jeshu, "for only my heavenly Parent, not any creature of flesh and blood, could have revealed it to you. So now I'll tell you something too: you are Rock, and it is on this Rock that I'll establish my community. No forces of hell will overcome it.

(continued on page 135)

3 The subsequent dialogue between Jeshu and Rock probably stems from Matthew's community, a community understanding itself as being under Petrine authority, the authority of Rock (whose Greek name is Peter). Since these verses praising Rock are found only in Matthew's gospel, we can safely presume that this is a primary reason that the emerging Petrine church (under Constantine's influence) chose to give this book its position of honor in the canon.

⚖ In the context of a late first-century debate about legitimate Christian authority, this gospel clearly comes down on the side of Rock's leadership. Whether this community is located in Antioch or somewhere else, it considers Jacob's community in Jerusalem too inflexible in matters of halacha and Paul's communities scattered around the Hellenistic world too lax. The Matthean community, and consequently this gospel, seek a middle road, one where Gentile converts are accepted but where all are bound by an authoritative structure of halachic observance.

4 Jeshu admonishes his disciples to keep his messianic identity a secret. This so-called messianic secret is inherited from Mark's gospel. One school of thought sees this secret as an element added by Mark to explain the absence of any authentic dominical sayings in which Jeshu claims to be the Messiah. Another school of thought believes that Jeshu actually said something like this. In that case, we must presume two things: first, that Jeshu did indeed consider himself to be God's anointed, and second, that he didn't want this term being misunderstood. After all, the normal understanding of a messiah would be a political figure, a David-like monarch who would throw off the yoke of Roman oppression. If Jeshu saw himself as God's anointed or Messiah, it was certainly not with this meaning.

5 This saying suggests that there is no choice about having or not having a cross; the only choice is about taking it up or not taking it up. A true spiritual path is never one of avoidance or denial. It leads through adversity, not around it. Obstacles there will always be, at least as long as there is still life in our ego. When the false self has dissolved

(continued on page 136)

I will give you the keys to the heavenly reign so that whatever you allow on earth will be allowed in heaven and whatever you forbid on earth will be forbidden in heaven."[3] Then Jeshu gave his disciples strict orders not to tell anyone that he was the Messiah.[4]

It was from this point on that Jeshu began to make it clear to his disciples that it was necessary for him to go up to Jerusalem; to suffer greatly there at the hands of the elders, the chief priests, and the Torah scholars; to be put to death; and on the third day to be raised up. Rock took him aside and began to protest: "Heaven help you, Lord, this kind of thing can't happen to you." Jeshu turned to Rock and said, "Get behind me, Satan. You're blocking my way. You're thinking about this too much from a human perspective rather than from a divine one." Then Jeshu said to his disciples, "If anyone wants to walk with me, that person must put aside his ego, take up his cross,[5] and follow me.

(continued on page 137)

into a surrender to the Divine, only then does the cross disappear. When the ego has been totally transformed into the true self, then all conflict is eliminated. For most of us, however, this occurs sometime after death.

6 The paradox of losing our life to gain our life is central to spiritual practice. The struggle is between the small self and the large self, the false self and the true self. The large self, the true self, is a self totally centered in the Divine, totally surrendered to the divine will. This entails a readiness to see any moment as the perfect situation for loving action, for compassion, for creativity. No time is spent lamenting what cannot be changed; one's energies are consumed in responding to the present moment in all its ineluctability. To experience this real self is to know the Divine. What good indeed is it to gain the whole world but lose the essence of what we are, since that essence is divine?

7 The image of the end-time judge coming on the clouds of heaven to dispense rewards and punishments seems almost puerile in comparison to the depth of the earlier teachings. This scenario comes from the apocalyptic vision of Matthew's community. Paul too thought that he would be alive for that glorious day. It did not, however, come within Paul's lifetime—or Matthew's, for that matter. And that's because an end-time judge will never come on the clouds, since that coming is a spiritual reality, not something to be anticipated like an arriving train. Yes, our after-death experience will be affected by the choices we made in this life, and in that sense there is both judgment and reward or punishment. But there is no final division of people into winners or losers, because God will win in the end. We will all come to realize the larger divine reality of which we are a part—even the demons, if there indeed be any.

Those who want to keep their lives must be willing to let go of them. Those who let go of their lives because of me will find them.**6** What good is it, after all, if you gain the whole world but lose the essence of what you are? What are you willing to take in exchange for that which is most deeply you? For I'll be coming someday in the glory of my heavenly Parent, surrounded by my angels, and on that day I'll reward people according to what each one has done.**7** You can believe me when I say that there are people standing here today who will not see death before they see me coming in regal glory."

(*continued on page 139*)

8 | This scene is commemorated in the Christian holiday of the Transfiguration. Many scholars see this as a misplaced resurrection appearance. I tend to see it more as a darshan experience, something common in Hindu practice, when disciples sit in the presence of an enlightened person and experience this wordless presence as a blessing. When I first experienced a darshan with a guru, it was this scene in the gospel that came to mind for me. I find it entirely credible that the powerful presence of the divine mystery in Jeshu was sometimes manifested in forms of light. The experience of this light would certainly have upset Jeshu's disciples. We see this in Rock's confused wish to build *succoth,* or tents, for everyone—a hint that this scene may have occurred around the time of Succoth, the Feast of Tents, when Jews remember God's revelation during the forty years they wandered in the desert.

9 | This kernel of a darshan experience has been highly elaborated in the gospel tradition. The presence of Elijah and Moses symbolically validates the scriptural affirmation of Jeshu's messianic role. Moses symbolized the Torah, just as Elijah symbolized the Prophets; and those were the two parts of the Hebrew Bible that had been canonized—made normative—at this time. Thus, even in the gospels, the ordinary way of referring to the Bible is "the Torah and the Prophets" *(Torah v'neviim).* The text therefore presents us with a visual midrash by having Jeshu symbolically framed between the Torah and the Prophets, thoroughly ensconced, as it were, in biblical attestation.

10 | The discussion that ensues when they are walking down the hill stems from the community. It can best be understood as a response to the rabbinic Jews who challenged the members of Matthew's community, asking them how this Jeshu can be the Messiah if Elijah has not returned to be his proclaimer. The midrashic answer of Matthew's community was that the martyred Jochanan the Immerser had indeed been Elijah and had fulfilled his task of preparing the way for the proclamation of Jeshu as God's Messiah.

It was six days later when Jeshu took Rock, Jacob, and Jochanan (Jacob's brother) and led them up high onto a hill—just the four of them. There Jeshu was transformed before their very eyes: his face shone like the sun, and his clothes dazzled like daylight.[8] Moses and Elijah[9] appeared to them, too, and they were talking with Jeshu. Rock spoke to Jeshu and said, "Lord, it's good being here. If you'd like, I'll make three *succoth:* one for you, one for Moses, and one for Elijah." He hadn't finished the sentence when a bright cloud came over them, and a voice from the cloud said, "This is my child, a child whom I love, a child in whom I take great delight; listen to him." When the disciples heard this, they fell to the ground, overcome with fear. But Jeshu came up to them and, touching them, said, "Get up now, and don't be afraid." When they looked up, they saw no one there but Jeshu.

As they were coming down from the hill Jeshu ordered them not to talk about this vision with anyone until he was raised from the dead. His disciples asked him why the Torah scholars insist that Elijah must come first. Jeshu answered them, "Elijah does come first to begin the restoration of all things. But what I'm telling you is that Elijah has already come, and people didn't recognize him, treating him any way it suited them. And I will suffer too at the hands of those same people."[10] It was then that the disciples realized that he had been talking to them about Jochanan the Immerser.

(*continued on page 141*)

11 What a change in scene. Jeshu comes down from the mountain where God is experienced in ecstasy to the valley of tears where God is experienced in the pain of the world. This valley of tears has long been a part of Christian experience and Christian prayer. *"In hac lacrimarum valle"* (in this valley of tears) is a poignant phrase from the *Salve Regina* (Hail Holy Queen), the prayer that is always chanted before the statue or icon of Mary at the end of the monastic day.

12 We see in this story the juxtaposition of physical ailment and demonic possession. An epileptic seizure would certainly have looked like demonic possession to Jeshu's contemporaries—and perhaps to Jeshu himself. His cure of the boy is immediate, and we learn from the subsequent query of his disciples that they had earlier tried to cast out this spirit of illness, though unsuccessfully. Jeshu points them to the reality of trust. Both the folksy analogy of the mustard seed and the humorously hyperbolic nature of the trope involving moving mountains seem to breathe the spirit of Jeshu. It is, in other words, an authentic part of the hidden gospel.

13 "Faith can move mountains" has become an aphorism of Christian piety, but what does it really mean? This is not simply an encouragement of the magical type of wish fulfillment that psychologists connect with childhood. This teaching affirms the spiritual connectedness of all reality. When we are aware of that connectedness, then influence passes easily from one center to another, and healing follows very naturally as well. But when our ego tightens around the illusion of separateness, then little of that energy is available for helping or healing others. If we can trust the divine reality, the reign of God, then mountains of internal struggle and pain are indeed moved for ourselves and for those around us. The disciples had obviously not yet learned how to access that reality; thus, Jeshu's instruction here seems consonant with his basic message of being open to God's reign and trusting its extraordinary power.

When the four of them had returned to where the crowds were,[11] a man came up to Jeshu and, kneeling before him, said, "Lord, have compassion on my son. For he is an epileptic and suffers terribly from seizures that lead to his frequently falling into fire or water.[12] I even brought him to your disciples, but they weren't able to heal him." Jeshu answered, "This is a generation of people without trust and profoundly lost. How long am I to be with you? How long am I to put up with you? Bring the boy here to me." Jeshu then spoke harshly to the demon, who immediately left the boy, with the result that he was healed in that very hour.

Afterward, when the disciples were alone with Jeshu, they asked him why they were unable to cast out the demon. He answered them, "It's because of your lack of trust. Believe me when I tell you that if your trust were no larger than a mustard seed, you could ask this hill to move from one place to another.[13] With just that small amount of trust, nothing would be impossible for you."

While they were still together in the Galilee, Jeshu said to the disciples, "I will be handed over to people who will kill me, but on the third day I will be raised." They were very upset when they heard this.

(continued on page 143)

14 Jeshu did not pay the temple tax for Rock and himself by having Rock catch a fish with money in its mouth. That would be precisely the kind of foolishness Jeshu rejected in the temptations following his immersion in the Jordan by Jochanan. It is more than likely that Jeshu did not pay the tax at all, and that is probably what led to these tax-collectors' concern in the first place. After all, Jeshu was an itinerant, without a fixed address, house, or land. Even in our own world, it is difficult to tax the homeless. What is missing in the transmission of this story is the simple word *if*. In other words, Jeshu really said that *if* Rock were to catch a fish with the right amount of money in its mouth, then that would suffice to pay the temple tax for both of them. We can readily imagine the peasants standing around breaking into laughter.

⚖ The teaching of Jeshu in this story is both politically revolutionary and profoundly theological. Jeshu refuses to identify himself or his people as victims of the oppressive system of Roman occupation. They remain free citizens, not vassals of Rome. They are the legitimate citizens in a kingdom unjustly occupied by the totalitarian Roman regime. Jeshu is deeply conscious of his freedom. Given his itinerant lifestyle and consequent lack of possessions, he embodies the freedom of the wanderer, the man on the open road. This lifestyle also connects him with his ancestors, who wandered in the wilderness for forty years as free people after their escape from Egyptian slavery and before their entrance into the Promised Land.

15 The role of the child stands central in Jeshu's teaching. Children live closer to the spiritual world from which they have recently come; their doors of perception are less overlaid with the grids of accumulated habit and bias. When my son was a little boy and felt that he was not getting enough of my attention, he would grasp my chin in his hands and say to me, "Put your face right here!" And once when I was playing in the sandbox with my daughter, my mind was wandering in other directions. My daughter, like a Zen roshi, pulled at my pants and said, "Dad, we're in the sandbox now." Children can be our greatest spiritual teachers, and Jeshu was well aware of that.

When they arrived at Kapharnahum, some tax-collectors came to Rock and asked, "Doesn't your master pay the Temple tax?" "Of course he does," said Rock. But when he got home, before he could say anything, Jeshu asked him, "What's your opinion on this matter, Shimon? From whom do the kings of this earth collect tribute or tax—from their own citizens or from foreigners?" "From foreigners," answered Shimon. "Then I guess the citizens are tax free," said Jeshu. "Nevertheless, we don't want to cause any trouble, so go to the lake and throw in a line. Take the first fish you catch, and when you open its mouth, you'll find a coin. Use the coin to pay the Temple tax for both of us."[14]

The disciples came to Jeshu at this time, asking him, "Who is the greatest where God reigns?" Calling a small child[15] to his side and placing him in the middle of his disciples, Jeshu said to them, "Believe me when I tell you that unless you turn your lives around and become like children, you'll never know God's reign. For the greatest where God reigns is the one with the receptivity of this little child. And those who are open to receive a small child like this in my name are open to receive me as well.

(continued on page 145)

16 The discourse continues with an angry reflection on those who cause children to stumble. Perhaps at this point we are seeing the intervention of the community into this narrative. It could well be, too, that the topic has shifted from children to the "little ones" who constitute Matthew's community, especially those who are still young in their faith. In that case, it might be the Pharisees who are once again coming under fire, this time for challenging the members of the Jeshu movement for their departure from the pharisaic teaching that is increasingly becoming normative Judaism in the latter decades of the first century.

⚠ It is impossible to read these words today without a sense of profound sadness for the betrayal and abuse of children in our society. Children molested by clergy are doubly victims, first by the priest predators and second by the complicit bishops who failed to protect them and other potential victims. Victims too are the millions of other children physically abused by parents or caregivers, psychologically abused by the neglect and indifference of their society. It is a tragic irony that leads us to cruelty toward these young people, from whom we could learn most about the true meaning of life.

17 The strong statements about hands, feet, and eyes becoming obstacles and the necessity of removing them reminds us that whatever holds us back from God and God's reign must be removed. Once we are clear about our ultimate concern, our primary reason for being, then anything hindering our movement in that direction must be eliminated. Jeshu was not, of course, talking about physical surgery. Here, as everywhere in the scriptures, literalism is the primary enemy of meaning. What Jeshu refers to here includes the grasping symbolized by the hand, the running off in our own ego directions symbolized by the foot, and the craving for things outside of ourselves represented by the eye.

18 The "fiery death" alluded to in this text need not represent an eternal hell, although this is certainly an image Jeshu might have used for the after-death consequences of the choices we make in this present

(continued on page 146)

But those who become obstacles for even one of these little ones who trusts me—such people are better off drowning in the depths of the sea with a millstone tied around their neck.**16** Damn the world because of the obstacles placed in front of people trying to be God-centered, and damn the person responsible for those obstacles, even though I know such obstacles are bound to occur.

"So if one of your hands or feet becomes an obstacle for you, cut it off and discard it. You're better off entering into life without a hand or foot than being thrown into eternal fire with both hands and feet. And even if one of your eyes becomes an obstacle for you, cut it out and throw it away, too.**17** You're still better off entering into life with only one eye than being thrown into a fiery death with eyes intact.**18**

(continued on page 147)

life. I cannot affirm a universe in which anyone can be eternally separate from God or one in which either a human being or a demon could eternally thwart God's will. The great traditions affirm an after-death transformation, but the images suggesting its reality—such as resurrection, reincarnation, heaven, hell, and purgatory—should be handled lightly, not literally. The primary thrust of this teaching of Jeshu—as indeed of all his teachings—points to the present moment, not to some after-death plane of experience.

△ The real import of Jeshu's teaching here is not the existence of guardian spirits. What he really stresses is the importance of every human being, especially the young and vulnerable. People in our society who merit FBI bodyguards are considered important. So if each of us, even those of least importance in the eyes of the world, has a guardian angel to help us along our spiritual path, then we are indeed of immense importance in this universe.

19 The parable of the lost sheep certainly comes from Jeshu. The simple story forcefully portrays the overwhelming love of a God for whom each individual carries the value of all creation. This parable demonstrates as well Jeshu's own special love for the marginalized, the outcast, the ones who in the natural order of things will always be overlooked. A German proverb admonishes us to "butter the edges of the bread, because the middle will always get enough." This admonition makes as much sense in our time as it did in the life-world of Jeshu.

"See to it that you don't despise one of these little ones, for I'm telling you that they have their own angels in heaven who see the face of my heavenly Parent continually.

"Give me your opinion of this situation. If someone has a hundred sheep and one of them wanders off, won't he leave the ninety-nine others on the hillside and go after the stray? And if he finds the wandering sheep, you can believe me when I tell you that he'll feel more joy on that account than because of the ninety-nine who remained on the hillside. The situation is the same with your heavenly Parent: he doesn't want to lose even one of these little ones.[19]

(*continued on page 149*)

20 The remaining verses seem to be products of the community, useful instructions for maintaining order and for dealing with the failures of community measures. The steps outlined make sense in any community or workplace today. Public criticism of another is bad policy at any level; taking the person aside for a private conversation softens any words of criticism that need to be spoken. A Jewish teaching admonishes us never to criticize a person in public and thus bring "color to his or her face."

21 Continued recalcitrance invites a larger setting in which the person can see that the criticism does not stem from the idiosyncratic perspective of one community member alone. The abandonment of the person after the failure of the second type of intervention might be seen today as a kind of "tough love." The aspersions cast on Goyim, non-Jews, and tax-collectors suggest that Matthew's community has already lost some of the compassion of its founder.

22 The final verses also seem to stem from the community's reflection on its current life-world. Matthew's community had its own body of halacha. The teaching on the greater efficacy of prayer when there is cooperation in petition seems consistent with what we learn in all the major traditions. The final phrase is an adaptation of a rabbinic statement that God is present wherever two or three gather together and study Torah. This is consonant with the way Matthew's community sees in Jeshu the new Torah, the messianic halacha.

23 Rock's query provides a wonderful illustration of the difference between a literal and a spiritual approach to reality. Religious bureaucrats in every tradition want to reduce the teaching to quantifiable units. Shall I forgive seven times or perhaps eight times? Jeshu, like a practiced Zen master, tries to break through this kind of mind-set by exploding this whole way of thinking. Not eight times, not nine times, but seventy times seven. In other words, Jeshu attempts to explode Rock's consciousness into a different order of understanding, one not bound by such quantitative limits. As in so many parallel instances, Jeshu is prompting his disciples to a quantum leap of consciousness.

"If a brother or sister falls short of your standards, go and talk with that person, just the two of you. If the person is open to what you're saying, then you've won back that brother or sister.[20] But if the person is not open, take one or two others with you, so that everything said can be confirmed by the testimony of two or three witnesses. If this doesn't work, then take the matter to the community, but if even the community is ignored, then treat the person as you would any of the Goyim or tax-collectors.[21]

"Believe me when I tell you that whatever you forbid on earth will be forbidden in heaven, and whatever you allow on earth will be allowed in heaven. Let me say this again: if two of you on earth are in agreement about anything you're praying for, that prayer of yours will be answered by my heavenly Parent. In fact, wherever two or three of you come together in my name, I am right there with you."[22]

It was about this time that Rock came to Jeshu and asked, "Lord, how many times am I supposed to forgive a brother or sister who falls short of my standards? As much as seven times?" Jeshu said to him, "I wouldn't say seven but seventy times seven.[23] Let me explain this to you in a story about God's reign. Once there was a king who decided to check on the financial records of his servants. As he was in the process of doing this, one of them was brought in who owed him thousands. Since this servant had no way of paying, the king decided to have him sold as a slave, along with his wife and children and all his possessions, so that the debt could be paid. At that point the servant, falling at the king's feet, begged for pity and promised to repay every cent. Having compassion on the servant, the king not only let him go but canceled the debt.

(continued on page 151)

24 This parable further illustrates that forgiveness is not a luxury we can engage in now and then, or up to a measurable number of times. It is the very lifeblood of the spiritual life, the way in which we maintain our connection with the flow of divine energy. As soon as we try to limit it in any way, we cut ourselves off from God's reign, from the whole realm in which prayer derives its efficacy and healing its solace. The story dramatically highlights the absurd contradiction into which we fall when we are willing to receive continually the forgiveness of God but dispense forgiveness to our neighbor in a calculating and miserly manner.

25 Certain codas and caveats seem in order here. Forgiveness of the other does not mean perpetuating a situation in which we do not show proper respect and love for ourselves. We can be open to another's growth, recognize the future saint in every sinner, and nevertheless need to affirm our own growth by removing ourselves from that person's presence. Some relations are toxic, and we need to be able to recognize that. There is nothing masochistic in the teachings of Jeshu, and it is sad that they are sometimes interpreted that way. Forgiveness keeps affirming future for the other, just as we count on God to continually affirm future for us. It trusts that God's love is great enough to bridge any past failure and create thereby a new path to wholeness and healing. The extent to which we block that openness in any of our dealings with others—and incidentally in any of our dealings with ourselves as well—causes us to fall out of the unity consciousness connecting us with the Divine.

"But on the way out, running into a fellow servant who owed him a hundred, he grabbed him and started to choke him, demanding that he pay up every cent. The man fell at his feet and begged for pity, promising to repay him, but he refused to listen and went off to have him thrown in jail for as long as the debt was unpaid. The other servants were very upset when they heard about this, and they went off to tell the king the whole story. The king, of course, had him brought in immediately and said to him, "You are one rotten servant! I canceled your whole debt when you asked me. Don't you think you should have shown some compassion to your fellow servant as I did to you?" Hot with anger, the king turned him over to be tortured until he paid back all that he owed.[24] And this is how my heavenly Parent will deal with each one of you if you don't show sincere forgiveness to your brothers and sisters."[25]

1 This exchange about divorce highlights two important features of Jeshu's message. We note his use of the Genesis text about man and wife becoming one flesh. This points to Jeshu's unity consciousness, the nondualistic space his soul inhabits, symbolized by the primordial mythic garden in which our first parents lived. This is synonymous with Jeshu's central teaching about God's reign. In inviting us to receive God's reign, Jeshu invites us to be open to ever-larger spaces of consciousness until we come to the nondual consciousness which he habitually inhabits. God reigns where we do God's will, and we do God's will when we live fully with a consciousness expanded to the parameters of the world God created in the beginning, the garden where all God's creatures live together in peace. In other words, God's reign entails a perfect unity of consciousness and conscience, of loving openness to the Divine and of compassionate outreach to the neighbor.

⚘ In Jeshu's time, women were essentially possessions in a male home, transferred from father's home to husband's home. After divorce, women often fell between the cracks of societal protection and ended up as prostitutes, social pariahs in almost every culture. Restricting the grounds for divorce to blatant sexual misconduct protected women from the insecurity of having husbands dismiss them for burning dinner.

2 Eunuchs are castrated men. In my translation, I enlarged the term into the phrase "those who are incapable of marriage." In Catholic circles this text is often used as a support text for celibacy, whether in the priesthood or in religious orders. This really misses the point. In a Jewish context, it invites men to remain single after divorce rather than seek another marriage. The Essenes followed such a halachic injunction not to remarry—a law peculiar to their own sect. Is Jeshu then asking men who have divorced their wives to remain as unmarried widowers? If so, it would be yet another small link to a possible Essenic background for Jeshu.

It would seem that widowed and divorced men would want to enjoy once again the blessings of an intimate relationship. Perhaps Jeshu uses

(continued on page 154)

9 □ On the Road to Jerusalem
(Matthew 19:1–20:34)

Afterward, when he had finished saying all this, Jeshu left the Galilee and went into the territory of Judea that lies beyond the Jordan River. Large crowds followed him there, and he healed them. Meanwhile, some Pharisees approached him and put him to the test by asking him whether or not it was lawful to divorce one's wife for any reason. "Haven't you read that in the beginning the Creator made human beings male and female?" Jeshu answered them. "And this is the reason that a husband, after leaving his father and mother, clings to his wife so that the two of them become one flesh, so that they really are not two but one flesh. So no one should try to separate what God has joined." "Why, then," they asked, "did Moses allow a husband to give his wife divorce papers and be rid of her?" Jeshu replied, "It was because of your hardheartedness that Moses allowed you to divorce your wives, but that's not how it was in the beginning. I'm telling you now that anyone who divorces his wife (except for sexual immorality), and marries another woman, commits adultery."[1]

His disciples said to him, "If that's how things are between husband and wife, it doesn't make any sense to get married." Jeshu replied, "Not everyone can grasp this teaching but only those who can receive it as a gift. For some are incapable of marriage[2] from the day of their birth; others are incapable of marriage because of what others have done to them; and yet others have made themselves incapable of marriage for the sake of God's reign. This is a teaching you can receive only when you're ready for it."

(continued on page 155)

this injunction to test the seriousness of a man's intention to divorce. In other words, if he knows that he will not marry again, a man might be hesitant to enter upon a divorce unless there is truly no other alternative. In that case, Jeshu's teaching, rather than presenting binding halacha, mere external legal structure, might be a means of establishing seriousness of intent, his natural concern as a teacher of *kavanah,* or intentionality. "Think about never marrying again," Jeshu is telling these men, "and then decide whether or not you truly want to pursue a divorce."

Jeshu walks into the gospel narrative as a single man living without a spouse, despite the requirement of marriage within his society. Was he widowed or divorced? We have no evidence either way. Had he spent time with the Essenes? Does that account for his apparently celibate state? Was he unmarried simply because peasant life was so poor that marriage was not feasible? Was his single state a protest against the patriarchal model typified by the family of the time? Was Jeshu homosexual, finding intimacy with his "beloved disciple"? Did he enjoy a "common-law marriage" with Mary Magdalene? Was Jeshu's sex life simply expunged from the records with the result that his portrait is agenital? All of these scenarios have been argued, but none with enough evidence to lead to consensus. Whatever the truth about Jeshu's sexuality, we can presume that it was embraced with the truth, love, and compassion that characterized all else he did and said.

| 3 | The paragraph about Jeshu and the children exemplifies that unity consciousness so prevalent throughout his teachings. One is reminded of the beautiful but somewhat enigmatic teaching attributed to Jeshu in the Gospel of Thomas (saying 37) that people whose lives have been transformed by the divine truth will be able to take their clothes off and lay them down in a field as children do when they play.

The fuller consciousness characterizing God's reign finds itself mirrored in the child's view of everything as new and wonderful. This paradise consciousness (another term for unity consciousness) links us to our mythical first parents in their primordial garden world. Such a

(continued on page 156)

At this time some people brought children to Jeshu so that he could place his hands on them and pray for them. The disciples were complaining about this when Jeshu said, "Let the children come to me. Don't try to keep them away. They're what God's reign is all about." And so Jeshu placed his hands on the children and then continued on his way.[3]

(continued on page 157)

garden, however, lies not in space—a piece of geography yet to be discovered or excavated—but in the consciousness that shapes and defines our experience.

We can enter this garden and experience God's reign at any moment if only we can find "the gateless gate" and awaken to our true identity. However, following the paradoxical character of so many spiritual teachings, we find this gate only by not seeking it, by simply surrendering ourselves to that larger consciousness where God (not the ego) reigns.

4 We know that things are going wrong from the first words of the dialogue. The young man asks what he can do to gain eternal life. In other words, he sees the goal of religious practice as an object, something he can acquire through a quid pro quo arrangement, a good deed in exchange for eternal life. Whether or not he wants to call that object heaven or nirvana, eternal life or the world to come, the question itself reveals a form of spiritual materialism, an understanding of spiritual goals analogous to material objects to be acquired. Is he perhaps seeking to add yet another trophy to his collection?

This mentality, a very common one today, is a "gumball" approach to religion. We want to put in our quarter and get the gumball. This "quarter" might be confessing with our lips that Jesus is Lord, reciting the magic prayer of Jabez, chanting a magic phrase, having a strongly emotional religious experience, seeing the pope, kissing a sacred relic, or any of countless other "quarters" jingling in our pockets as we hear the call of the religious hawkers. Authentic spirituality sees all of these as aberrations, luring us from the path where we must do our own practice and, in the words of the Buddha, be lamps unto ourselves.

5 Jeshu tries, but ultimately fails, to deflect this young man's attention either from himself (Jeshu) or from some gimmick. "Why are you asking me about good deeds? Only God is good." How seldom these words are chosen for sermons or Bible classes. Many Christians find themselves embarrassed by a Jeshu directing attention away from himself, pointing to God instead. Is not Jeshu after all God? Only in the mystical sense that we all are. Jeshu, after all, is different from us in

(continued on page 158)

And now a young man stepped up to Jeshu and said, "Teacher, what good deed must I do to gain eternal life?"**4** Jeshu replied, "Why are you asking me about good deeds? Only God is good. But as for your desire to enter into life, observe the *mitzvot.*"**5** "Which ones?" asked the young man. Jeshu replied: "Don't murder; don't commit adultery; don't steal; don't tell lies about others; respect your parents; and love your neighbor as yourself."

(continued on page 159)

degree, not in kind. A fundamental Christian mistake has been to understand Jeshu as an object of worship instead of a model for emulation. The traditional Christian teaching states that he is fully human and fully divine. Most Christians, however, understand that to mean that he is fully divine *despite* being fully human. The truth is that he is fully divine precisely *because* he is fully human.

6 The young man had asked about "gaining" eternal life, thus betraying his acquisitive nature even in spiritual matters. Jeshu's modification of the question suggests more of a process or a becoming than a quantity and a possession. Realizing that the young man is not responding to the initial invitations to spiritual awakening and growth, Jeshu makes a final effort to help him drop his quantitative way of thinking and be open to the radical nature of discipleship. Jeshu asks the young man to give everything to the poor, thereby acquiring great wealth in his interior life, and follow him. This young man is in no way up to that kind of challenge. He goes away sad, because he can neither imagine parting with his current wealth nor envision the future spiritual wealth he could have in a conscious and centered life. At one level, we can say that Jeshu failed that day. But the real failure in the story belongs to the young man. He remains, like Lot's wife turned to salt, a symbol of our human ability not to recognize the divine call.

7 Jeshu claims that camels get through needles' eyes more easily than wealthy people enter God's reign. The outlandish character of the hyperbole seems thoroughly consonant with the tenor of rhetoric in the Middle East, as well as with Jeshu's rich humor. The message is clear. Wealth can obstruct our spiritual growth. This can happen in three ways: how it is acquired, how it is related to, and how it is used.

The young man answered, "I have observed all of these commandments. What do I still need to do?" Jeshu said to him then, "If you want to be fully alive, go and sell everything you have, and give it to the poor. That will put all your wealth in heaven. Then come back and follow me."**6** Hearing this teaching, the young man went away sad, because he was very wealthy.

Jeshu then said to his disciples, "Believe me when I tell you that it's not easy for the wealthy to enter God's reign. I would even go so far as to say that a camel might have a better chance of getting through the eye of a needle than a rich person has of entering God's reign."**7** When the disciples heard this they were very upset, and they asked Jeshu how anyone could be saved. Jeshu looked at them and said, "This isn't something human beings can do, but God can do anything."

(continued on page 161)

8 | Matthew brings the chapter to a close in a way that reflects more of his life-world than that of Jeshu. The early Christians often gave up much earthly wealth and security to join the nascent community. The Jeshu of this text assures them a place in history's final act. When the end-time comes, they will sit on twelve thrones judging the twelve tribes of Israel. The life-world here is not that of Jeshu but the much narrower one of the early church.

⚖ | One discerns that bit of resentment and revenge that begins to characterize subsequent Christianity and is all too present in many Christian communities today—something the Germans call *Schadenfreude,* a delight in the sufferings of others. Registering other people on the lists of hell continues to be a Christian practice in certain circles; even Dante succumbed to the temptation. But the origin of this kind of thinking in the teachings of Jeshu seems dubious.

9 | Matthew has deliberately placed this parable after the previous teachings on riches, for the story reflects the immoral practice of the wealthy landowners who hired laborers one day at a time so that they could drive their wage according to the availability of unemployed workers. The background of this parable, a marketplace teeming with the unemployed, certainly paints a bleak picture of first-century Palestine's economy. The wage received for a day's work could normally feed a working man and his family for two days at most; after that he had to find another job or resort to stealing or begging.

Such a rapacious landowner hardly seems an appropriate figure for Jeshu to use to illustrate the way God acts in the world. And yet that may well be part of the power of Jeshu's teaching examples. Did he not also say (Matthew 7:1–12) that if we humans, limited as we are, manage for the most part to do good things for our children, then how much more so does God know how to take care of God's children? Could it be, then, that the example of a typically unjust landowner nonetheless becomes a mirror in which we can see, dimly reflected, qualities found with much greater clarity and purity in God?

At this point, Rock said to Jeshu, "Look at us. We've given away everything to follow you. What's in store for us?" Jeshu then said to the disciples, "Believe me when I say this to all of you who have followed me: in the new creation, when I sit on my throne of glory, you who have followed me will also sit on twelve thrones, judging the twelve tribes of Israel. And everyone who has left homes or siblings or parents or property for the sake of my name will receive all that a hundred times over and will inherit eternal life as well. Keep in mind, however, that many who are first now will be last then, and many who are last now will then be first."**8**

"Let me tell you something about God's reign through a story. Once there was a landowner who went to town**9** at daybreak to hire workers for his vineyard. After he had reached an agreement with some workers for a full day's wages, he put them to work in his vineyard. Going back to town at about nine o'clock that same morning, he found some other workers standing around idle, and he asked them to work in his vineyard, too, promising to pay them a fair wage. They agreed and went to work. Going back to town at noon and then in the middle of the afternoon, he did the same thing. At about five that afternoon, he went to town a final time and, finding more workers standing around, he asked them why they weren't working. They told him that no one had hired them, so he sent them into the vineyard with all the rest.

(continued on page 163)

10 As ruthless as the landowner in this story may be, he has decided on this particular day to be generous with those who were hired last. A coin called a denarius in the original text names the monetary equivalent of a normal day's wages. The landowner had quoted this wage to the ones hired first. He promised a fair wage to the ones hired second—without, however, actually naming an amount. The workers hired last were simply told to go to work. Only the first group knew what to expect. The second group no doubt expected half of a denarius. The third group had no idea what their recompense would be, probably a mere pittance for such a short time of actual labor. Perhaps they would receive simply some bread and a bowl of the lentil soup often served to workers. At pay time, all three groups were surprised. The latter two groups were delighted that they too received a full day's wage. Those in the first group, however, were understandably disappointed that they had not received more.

11 The complaints of the workers who had borne the heat of that day are not without meaning. They had, however, no objective grounds for complaint; they did receive what they had been promised. If the landowner chooses to be generous with those who worked only part of the day, is that not his prerogative? The point of the story echoes Jeshu's encounter with the rich young man who wanted to quantify what was required of him to achieve eternal life. This kind of calculation, however, does not reflect the ways in which the spiritual life works. The parable ends with the punch line that although the "last hired" would normally be looked on as society's losers, they are not losers in God's eyes. For the last shall be first, and the first last.

"When evening came, the landowner told his paymaster to call the workers in and pay them their wages, beginning with the last ones hired and ending with the ones hired at daybreak. When the ones who were hired at five that afternoon came up, they were paid a full day's wages. By the time the ones hired early in the morning came up, they were expecting to be paid more. But they too received a day's wages.[10] After receiving the pay, they complained to the landowner: 'These last people you hired worked only one hour, but you've paid them the same wages that we received, and yet we've been out there working and sweating in the sun all day.' The landowner said to one of them, 'I haven't cheated you, my friend. Didn't you agree to work for a full day's wages? Take what you've earned and go home. I want to pay these workers hired last the same as you. Aren't I free to do what I want with my money? It's no skin off your nose if I choose to be generous.' So it is that the last will be first and the first last.[11]

(continued on page 165)

12 The prophecy of Jeshu's death and resurrection comes from the early community. Perhaps Matthew fails to realize that when he portrays Jeshu as seeing the details of his future, he deprives him of his true humanity. Many of us grew up with this image of a divine Jeshu play-acting his earthly role, always reading the script to check his lines for the next scene. There was a time when Christians thought that this honored Jeshu, but today we realize how insulting it is. How can we truly identify with someone who is only playing a role, someone untroubled by the terrible insecurity that defines our human condition? This stems from a dualistic perspective in which the Divine can be understood only as the opposite of everything human. The contrary view, that the more fully human we are, the more divine we are, escaped the early Christian writers and many of the later Christian writers as well. Each successive gospel further diminishes Jeshu's humanity. Mark's Jeshu is the most human, Matthew's and Luke's less so, while John's Jeshu moves through life like a divine being pretending to be human.

13 This story reflects the early church's power struggles. Jacob, Shimon, Thomas, Mary Magdalene—the early texts show various contenders for authority in the early community. The context of the story entails Jeshu reigning in a messianic scenario, where he has the prerogative of assigning seats around his throne. How foreign this seems to anything Jeshu would really want. Dynasty building was hardly his goal. These scenes, however, with all their accompanying violence and bloodshed, filled the imagination of those less spiritually evolved than their teacher. The story mirrors the tiresome squabbles for power in the early church.

As Jeshu was going up to Jerusalem he took the twelve disciples aside privately and said to them while they walked along, "Pay attention. We are going up to Jerusalem, where I'll be handed over to the chief priests and Torah scholars, who will condemn me to death. They'll turn me over to the Goyim to be mocked, beaten, and crucified. But on the third day I'll be raised up."**12**

At this point, the mother of Zebedee's sons, approaching Jeshu with her sons, fell to her knees before him to ask a favor. Jeshu asked her what she wanted. She replied, "These are my two sons; promise me that where God reigns, they will sit on either side of you." "You don't know what you're asking," Jeshu answered her. "Can the two of you drink the cup I am about to drink?" "We can," answered the two brothers. Jeshu then said, "You will in fact drink my cup. As for sitting on either side of me, that's not my decision. Those places of honor are for those who have been assigned them by my heavenly Parent."**13**

(continued on page 167)

14 In this scene, we hear the authentic voice of Jeshu. For it was he who changed the concept of God's reign from the military defeat of enemies, delight in their horrible punishments, and ruling in their stead, to entrance into a larger consciousness of God's love and forgiveness. We see in Jeshu's words how that shift is rooted in a radical redefinition of power. It is not power *over* others, dominance, and control that open up the true meaning of authority, but power *for* others and service to them. Jeshu, after all, is the one who came to serve.

15 Postmodern philosophy reminds us that "to see is to see as." So much depends on the way we see the world and the situations confronting us from day to day. How did people see Jeshu then, and how do they see him today? Is he a deus ex machina, a divine being who comes down to fix a fallen humanity and then keep human beings in an infantile state of subservience? Or was his ministry to help us see that we are free, that we have power, that our deepest reality is divine? Perhaps the latter is why Jeshu's healing of the blind moves us so deeply. We too need to have our eyes opened. The old hymn reminds us, "I once was blind/ but now I see." Nothing happens in the spiritual life without this initial healing of our blindness, the opening of our eyes to a world that, in the words of the English Jesuit poet Gerard Manley Hopkins, is indeed "charged with the grandeur of God."

When the other ten disciples heard this conversation, they were angry with the two brothers. But Jeshu called them all together and said to them, "You all know how the leaders of the Goyim lord it over their subjects and how their big men like to throw their authority around. But this isn't how it's supposed to be with you. Whoever wants to be the big man among you should serve you, and whoever wants to be first among you should slave for you. After all, I didn't come to be served but to serve and to give my very life to help others."**14**

As they were leaving Jericho a large crowd followed Jeshu. Two blind men were sitting right there by the roadside. Hearing that Jeshu was passing by, they shouted, "Show compassion on us, Son of David." The crowd scolded them, telling them to be quiet but they only shouted all the louder: "Show compassion on us, Son of David." Hearing them, Jeshu stopped there in the road and said, "What do you want me to do?" "Lord, do something that will open our eyes," they answered. Moved with compassion, he touched their eyes, and immediately they could see again, and they followed after him.**15**

1 The glory of this "Palm Sunday" narrative begins with a fairy-tale prelude. We have seen other instances where the text of Matthew has picked up magical elements along the way—for example, in the story of finding a coin in the mouth of a fish. Here we are asked to believe that a chance stranger was simply told that Jeshu needed some animals and immediately acquiesced to the request. The community has probably forgotten an earlier relationship of Jeshu to certain people in Jerusalem who provided for his needs when he came south for the holidays. These Jerusalem connections account for other elements of the story as well, such as finding a place to stay in the crowded city during the pilgrimage festival of Passover.

2 The text describes two animals, not understanding Hebrew parallelism enough to realize that one animal is being named here, not two. The colt in the biblical quotation is not another animal but a literary repetition of the donkey. Understanding the text as referring to two animals leads to the humorous awkwardness we find in this text—people putting cloaks over the two animals and Jeshu apparently riding both of them at one time! Since the preponderance of evidence points to Matthew being Jewish, he may simply be passing on a story the way he received it, respectfully declining to correct his source.

3 The cadre of priests controlling the Temple were wealthy landowners who raised the animals being sacrificed there. Most of the Jewish pilgrims bought their sacrificial animals at the prices set by the priests. At the same time, since coins bearing images could not be brought within the Temple precincts, Jews from other countries had to exchange their currency for Temple shekels. Again it was the priests who established the rates of exchange.

Why did Jeshu focus on the tables of those selling pigeons? As a member of the destitute class, Jeshu, like most of his fellow Jews, had good reason to condemn these acts of injustice against the poor. The people offering pigeons might well feel less connected to God than the wealthy folks ahead of them offering bulls or rams. Perhaps the plight of the poor was uppermost in Jeshu's mind that day. Or perhaps

(continued on page 170)

10 □ Challenging the Religious Establishment (Matthew 21:1–23:39)

When they were near Jerusalem and had reached Beth-pageh by the Mount of Olives, Jeshu sent two of his disciples on an errand with these instructions: "Go into the village over there, and right away you will notice a donkey tied up with its colt. Untie them and bring them to me. And in case anyone asks you what you're doing, just say, 'The Lord has need of them.' The person will immediately let you have the animals.[1] All this happened so that the oracle of the prophet could be fulfilled: 'Tell the daughter of Zion: look how your king comes to you, humble, astride a donkey, a colt, the offspring of a beast of burden.'"

The disciples proceeded to do what Jeshu had asked. Bringing the donkey and the colt,[2] they threw their cloaks over them, and Jeshu climbed on. Most of the crowd threw their own cloaks in the road, and others, cutting down tree branches, placed them on the road, too. Crowds were running in front of Jeshu and behind him, and they were all shouting: "Save us now, Son of David. Blessings on the one who comes in the Lord's name. Save us now, heaven above!" And as Jeshu came into Jerusalem, everyone in the city wanted to know who he was. The crowds who were with him answered, "This is Jeshu, the prophet from Nazareth in the Galilee."

Then Jeshu went into the Temple and threw out all who were buying and selling things there; he overturned the tables of those who were exchanging currency and the chairs of those who were selling pigeons for sacrifice.[3]

(continued on page 171)

his message was that the Temple should be a place of prayer, not a center of business activities. People exchanging foreign coins and selling animals detracted from the Temple's essential nature. Or perhaps Jeshu saw a day when animal sacrifice would no longer be part of worshiping the God of Israel.

4 The story of the fig tree seems to have been badly patched together by the gospel author. We need to unpack its details. First we have the instance of the fig tree not producing fruit. Jeshu, remembering the words of Jeremiah (24:1–10), probably does point to the fruitless tree as an example of a people failing to turn to God and produce the fruits of a God-centered life. This is not the first time Jeshu uses the example of judging a tree by its fruit. Just as Jeremiah saw the coming destruction of the First Temple, so Jeshu sees the coming destruction of the Second Temple. In both cases the people are failing to live their covenantal life with God, seeking their security instead in their machinations either to oppose or to submit to the current world power: Babylon at the time of Jeremiah, Rome at the time of Jeshu.

5 Once the withering of the tree is in place as a parable, then Matthew has a bridge to the discussion of trust or faith. The conversation about faith is authentic and probably stems from Jeshu, but its context is skewed. Authentic faith has nothing to do with causing trees to wither or mountains to be moved. It does have to do, however, with the mountains of the mind. These are the mountains of despair that deep trust in God can cast into the sea. True faith will not cause trees to wither, but it may cause fruitless lives of despair to transform into fruitful lives of love and service.

He said to them, "It is written in the scriptures that my house will be called a house of prayer, but you have turned it into a den of robbers."

The blind and the crippled came to him there in the Temple, and he healed them. But when the chief priests and the Torah scholars saw the marvelous things he did and saw the children in the Temple shouting "Save us, Son of David!" they were furious. They said to him, "Do you hear what they're saying?" Jeshu replied, "Yes; don't you know the verse of scripture that says: 'You have made the lips of children, of babies at the breast, sing your praise'? With those words, Jeshu left them and went outside the city of Jerusalem to Beit-anyah, where he spent the night.

On his way back to the city, early the next morning, Jeshu was hungry. Seeing a lone fig tree[4] on the roadside, he went over to it but found nothing on it but leaves. He said to the tree, "May no fruit ever be found in your branches again!" The fig tree immediately withered. When the disciples saw this, they were amazed and asked Jeshu how it happened that the tree could wither so quickly. Jeshu answered them, "Believe me when I tell you this. If you have trust and are without doubt, not only will you be able to do what I did with the fig tree, but you'll even be able to tell a mountain to pick itself up and throw itself into the sea. If you only have trust, you'll receive anything you ask for in prayer."[5]

(continued on page 173)

6 The priests who challenge Jeshu represent a clerical type always present in the religious scene. They are, after all, collaborators with Rome. Not only do the towers of the Roman fortress, manned with archers, overlook the Temple courtyard, but the Roman authorities keep the priestly vestments and "grant" them to the clergy for the high holidays. These priests are men of divided consciousness, striving to please both God and Caesar, striving to be loyal both to God and to the "good lives" they enjoy at the expense of the Jewish peasantry.

7 The question of authority often divides religious communities. The truest spiritual authority is self-authenticating, stemming from profound mystical experience. Since self-deception remains a real possibility, even for those who have enjoyed enlightenment moments, there is a manifest need for a discerning community, a context in which spiritual experiences are tested. This is the purpose of a true guru, roshi, zaddik, staretz, or spiritual director as well as of communities of spiritual support and fellowship. People without the self-authentication of deep spiritual experience crave external support and are prone to root their religious truth in something other than their own experience.

8 We see this bureaucratic mentality in every religious organization. Bureaucrats, especially religious ones, never understand the self-authenticating authority of God's Spirit, the deep knowing that stems from mystical experience. Jeshu is portrayed here as playing their game, answering them in the categories of their own question, attempting to show them the ultimate fruitlessness and irrelevancy of this kind of discussion. The conversation ends on an almost humorous note in which Jeshu refuses to reveal his authority.

9 This chapter ends with two stories, one transparently clear and one confoundingly difficult. We begin with the easy one, the story of the two sons. It is another illustration of Jeshu's emphasis on the fruit that the tree bears. Words, creeds, titles, ritual incantations—all of these are meaningless unless they facilitate practice. God's reign belongs to those who do God's will. Something in our nature always seeks shortcuts. Can I lose

(continued on page 174)

Afterward, Jeshu came into the Temple, and while he was teaching there, the chief priests[6] and the elders of the people approached him, saying, "By whose authority are you doing these things? Who's given you permission?" Jeshu replied, "I want to ask you something first, and if you answer me, then I'll tell you by whose authority I'm doing these things.[7] What's the origin of Jochanan's practice of immersing people—is it something willed by God, or is its origin purely human?" They discussed this question among themselves, knowing that if they said his practice of immersing people was willed by God, then everyone would ask them why they didn't trust it; on the other hand, if they said this immersion rite was of purely human origin, then they had something to fear from the people, since they regarded Jochanan as a prophet. So they said to Jeshu, "We don't know." So he said to them, "Then I won't tell you by whose authority I'm doing these things."[8]

"What do you think about this story? A father had two sons.[9] He went to the first one and said, 'Son, go and work in the vineyard today.' But the son told him that he wouldn't do it, though later he changed his mind and went to work in the vineyard. Meanwhile, the father went to the second son and gave him the same command. 'Yes, sir,' he replied, but didn't go. Which of these two sons did what the father wanted?" They all answered, "The first." Then Jeshu said to them, "Believe me when I tell you that tax-collectors and prostitutes are going to enter God's reign before you. For Jochanan came to you walking the path of God-centeredness, and you didn't trust him, though the tax-collectors and the prostitutes trusted him. And yet, even when you saw that, you didn't change your mind and trust him.

(continued on page 175)

weight by taking a magic pill? Can I gain heaven by believing in my heart and saying with my lips that Jesus is Lord? If only there were something other than God's will, something easier, that we could do. If only, if only.

[⚘] Jeshu's message is clear in this parable of the two sons. Deeds, not creeds, open up for us the gateless gate. If religiosity fails to create kind and compassionate beings, then it is a sham and a pretense. The gentling of the heart cultivates the soil of the soul, enabling the divine seed to grow to a healthy harvest. That gentling happens in the give and take with our neighbor, those daily encounters in which we can love the other in the warm embrace of our compassion. It is in the vineyard of this world of daily affairs that the work of God is done and the will of God accomplished.

10 What a contrast in the second story. Here we find a spirit of revenge, of one-upmanship—the roots of a replacement theology that grows early in the soil of Christian consciousness; it teaches that the Christians are now the "true Israel" and that Judaism has been superseded or replaced by the Christian covenant. Is there any element in this second story that might indeed have come from the mouth of Jeshu? He certainly does call his fellow Jews to cleave to God in the covenantal life that has been revealed to them, to take care of one another during this time of oppression and suffering, to avoid worshiping or emulating the power of Caesar but not to resist it through armed conflict or guerrilla action. It is possible that he told a story of God's continuing efforts to give us the message that heals and calls to wholeness.

11 The ruthless and vengeful end of the story does not come from Jeshu. It better fits the growing resentment of the young community forming in his name. Many of the writings of the Christian Testament are tainted with an intolerance and prejudice toward the Jews and Judaism alike. Unfortunately, these early Christian texts do not breathe the spirit of their Master, for whom there were no enemies, no persecutors—only people seeking, with varying degrees of skill, the divine reality that they already are.

Listen to another story.[10] There was a landowner who planted a vineyard, put a fence around it, dug a hole for the winepress, and built a watchtower. He then turned it over to some tenant farmers while he traveled to another country. When the right time for picking the grapes drew near, he sent his servants to the tenant farmers to get the grape harvest. But the tenant farmers grabbed the servants, beat one, murdered another, and threw stones at a third. So the landowner sent other servants—more this time—and they did the same thing to them. Finally, he sent his son to them, figuring that they would respect him. But when the tenant farmers saw the son, they said to themselves, 'This is the son; if we kill him, we can inherit the whole estate.' So they grabbed him, threw him out of the vineyard, and murdered him. What do you think the owner of this vineyard is going to do to those tenant farmers when he comes home?" They answered him, "He'll kill those rotten tenant farmers, and he'll rent his vineyard to other tenant farmers who will deliver the grape harvest to him at the right time."[11] Jeshu said to them, "Didn't you ever read the verse of scripture that says: 'The very stone that the builders rejected has become the cornerstone; the Lord did this, and we think it's wonderful'? This is why I'm telling you now that God's reign will be taken from you and given to a people who will produce the right kind of fruit. Whoever stumbles on this stone will be injured, and whomever it falls on will be crushed." When the chief priests and the Pharisees heard these stories, they realized that Jeshu was talking about them. They wanted to arrest him, but they were afraid of the crowds, who looked on him as a prophet.

(continued on page 177)

12 This opening parable has clearly undergone some alteration in the telling during its move from the life-world of Jeshu to that of the early community. In its original setting it undoubtedly highlights the universalism of God's call, reaching beyond accepted categories of religious identity to those who are literally out on the streets. All are called to the feast, the great celebration of God's love. One can almost see the broad smiles on the peasant faces as they hear the story of invited guests missing a feast while hungry people on the street—people like themselves—rush in to fill the places at the food-laden tables.

13 The gospel writer, however, loads the story with another agenda: his own preoccupation with the rejection of the Jews and the election of the new people of God. The notion of people assaulting and killing the messengers who invite them to a feast seems preposterous. This theme has been introduced as a midrash on the destruction of Jerusalem and the Second Temple in 70 c.e., an act that many early Christians saw as "proof" that God was on their side and had indeed rejected the Jews. This story of narrowness and revenge in no way breathes the spirit of Jeshu; it seems to be a clumsy alteration of his story for purposes far less worthy.

14 The story of the coin of tribute almost certainly comes from Jeshu. In one sense, Jeshu has won this argument before it begins, when he challenges his interlocutor to show him the Roman coin of tribute. An observant Jew should not be carrying a coin bearing an image. When the man gives Jeshu one of these Roman coins, the crowd standing around almost certainly smiles, recognizing how Jeshu has already bested his opponent. After asking whose image the coin carries, Jeshu ironically comments that since the coin bears the emperor's image, it should be given back to the emperor. This dismissive comment indicates that paying taxes to Rome was not an issue that concerned him.

Jeshu spoke to them in parables once again. "Here is an image of God's reign. There was once a king who hosted a wedding reception for his son.¹² He sent his servants to call those who were invited to the reception, but the invited guests didn't want to come. A second time he sent servants with this message: 'Tell those who are invited that the banquet is prepared, the choicest foods are being served, and everything is ready to go, if they will just come to the reception.' But the intended guests still paid no attention to the invitation and went off on other errands: one to his farm, another to his business. Some of them actually apprehended the servants and beat them to death.¹³ The king was furious and sent his soldiers to execute the murderers and burn their city. Then the king said to his servants, 'The reception is still ready, but the guests I invited have proved unworthy. You'd better go out in the streets and invite anybody you find.' So the servants went out in the streets and brought in everyone they could find—people of every description—and the reception hall was finally filled with guests. But when the king came in to look at all the assembled guests, he saw someone there who wasn't wearing appropriate wedding attire. The king asked the man what he was doing at the reception without proper wedding attire, but the man had nothing to say. At that point, the king told the waiters to tie him up hand and foot and throw him outside in the dark, where he'll weep and grind his teeth in despair. For many are invited, but few are chosen."

After this, some of the Pharisees got together to talk about how they could trip Jeshu up in discussion. So they sent their disciples to him, along with some Herodians, with this question: "Teacher, we know that you're an honest person and that you teach the way of God in all sincerity. Give us your opinion then: is it lawful to pay taxes to the Roman Emperor or not?" Seeing right through their evil intentions, Jeshu said to them, "Why do you try to trick me, you religious phonies? Show me the tax money." They gave him a Roman coin.¹⁴

(continued on page 179)

15 This situation gives Jeshu the opportunity to say something that has real significance for him. Every Jew standing there knows the text of Genesis 1:26, which tells of God making humankind in God's image and likeness. So when Jeshu talks about giving to God what is God's, he discloses his mission to help everyone made in God's image—and that means every human being, not just the Jews—return to God. What better summarizes Jeshu's whole mission than his recognition of the divine image in every person and his desire that all people manifest that image fully, thereby accomplishing God's will and experiencing God's reign?

16 The question about resurrection rests on a confusion of religious metaphor and literalism. Then, as now, many people cling to the metaphor too literally, and this inevitably results in absurd discussions— avoiding organ transplants and questioning multiple marriages lest there be arguments over kidneys or spouses at the Last Judgment. The basic truth is that God is a God of the living, not of the dead. Abraham and Isaac are alive in God, and so are all of those who have passed on before us, and so will we be forever, for life is without end.

17 Since 613 *mitzvot* require some sort of prioritization, it was common to ask a young teacher what he considered to be the pivotal *mitzvot.* Jeshu answers with two Torah texts, one from Deuteronomy and one from Leviticus. In Mark's gospel, which Matthew is copying here, Jeshu begins his answer with the *She'ma,* the basic profession of Jewish faith that God is one. This had become so characteristic of Jewish life under the rabbis that Matthew wants to separate Jeshu from such a strong Jewish identity and thus drops that verse.

18 Bringing the two Torah texts together allows Jeshu to focus on the threefold love on which all life can be based: love of God, love of self, and love of neighbor. But Jeshu is not merely quoting scripture; he is interpreting it at the same time. The quotation he uses from Leviticus 19:18 ("You shall love your neighbor as yourself") is only the second half of the verse. The part Jeshu fails to quote reads: "You shall not take

(continued on page 180)

Then Jeshu said to them, "Whose image is on this coin and whose inscription?" "The emperor's," they replied. "Then give the emperor what belongs to the emperor," Jeshu said, "but give God what belongs to God."**15** They were stunned when they heard this answer, and they went away and left him alone.

It was on this same day that some Sadducees—who deny the resurrection of the dead—came to Jeshu with a question. "Teacher," they said, "Moses tells us that if a husband dies without offspring, his brother should marry his widow and have children to preserve the husband's family line. Now we once had in our community seven brothers. The oldest married but died without offspring, leaving his widow to his brother. The same thing happened with the second brother and then with the third brother, and finally with all seven. Finally, the woman herself died. In the resurrection of the dead,**16** which of these seven men will be her husband, since they were all married to her?" "You're missing the point," Jeshu said to them. "You don't understand the scriptures any more than you understand God's power. Those raised from the dead are not going to be marrying; they'll be like the angels in heaven. But regarding the resurrection from the dead, don't you know what's written for you in God's Word, 'I am the God of Abraham, and the God of Isaac, and the God of Jacob'? This is not a God of the dead but of the living." When the crowds heard this teaching, they were impressed.

When the Pharisees heard how Jeshu shut up the Sadducees, they got together, and one of them tried to trick him with a question. "Teacher," he asked, "what's the greatest commandment in the Torah?"**17** Jeshu replied, "You are to love the Lord your God with all your heart, with all your soul, and with all your mind. This is the first and most important commandment. The second is much like it: you are to love your neighbor as you love yourself. All of the scriptures hinge on these two commandments."**18**

(continued on page 181)

vengeance or bear a grudge against any *of your people ...*"(emphasis mine). So you may take vengeance, bear a grudge, and not love those who are not your people. You should not, however, take vengeance, bear a grudge, or fail in love to your own people. By leaving out the first part of the verse, Jeshu implicitly extends the mandate (love your neighbor) to all humankind.

19 Without doubt, Jeshu leveled a critique at the religious leadership of his day. Would he be any less critical with the religious leadership of our day? The first verses point to the gap that so often exists between preaching and practice in the clerical world. Televangelists shed tears about their desperate need for funds to do God's work while using the donated monies to build swimming pools. Corrupt bishops shuffle pedophile priests from parish to parish, victimizing the children they are mandated to protect.

20 In the next set of three injunctions, one at least seems to stem from Jeshu, namely, the words about calling no one on earth "father." Although this simple injunction stands out as one of Jeshu's most radical and profound teachings, it was never taught in the Roman Catholic world in which I was socialized—a world where every third person was called "Father" and the visible head of the church was a bishop in Rome called "Papa."

⚭ Jeshu lived in a patriarchal culture, a world where women were defined as extensions of male identity and male needs. The Talmud, the extensive commentary on the Torah, treats women as daughters, wives, and mothers—always in their relationship to men. In denying the role of the earthly father, Jeshu asserts that we are all brothers and sisters, our only Parent being our heavenly One.

Then, while the Pharisees were still gathered around him, Jeshu asked them, "What is your opinion about the Messiah? Whose son is he?" "David's," they answered. "Then tell me," Jeshu said to them, "why the inspired David calls him Lord when he writes in one of the Psalms: 'The Lord said to my Lord, sit here at my side, until I have subdued your enemies.' If David calls the Messiah Lord in this text, how can he be David's son?" No one was able to give Jeshu an answer to this question, and after that day no one dared to ask him any more questions at all.

After this, Jeshu spoke to a crowd that included his own disciples: "The Torah scholars and the Pharisees are your official religious teachers. You should, therefore, obey and follow everything they teach. But don't imitate their practice, because they don't practice what they preach.[19]

"They create heavy burdens to put on other people's backs, but you won't see them lifting a finger to help. Everything they do is for show. They make their *tefillin* broad and their *tzitzit* long. They seek out the places of honor at formal dinners and the best seats in the synagogues. They love the recognition they receive in public places when others call them rabbi.

"Now you shouldn't call anyone your rabbi, because you have only one Rabbi, and you are all brothers and sisters. And you shouldn't call anyone on earth your father, because you have only one Father, and he is in heaven.[20] And you shouldn't call anyone on earth your leader, because you have only one Leader, the Messiah.

(*continued on page 183*)

21 This teaching returns to the topic of legitimate models of authority. Jeshu's audience knew the collaborationist policies of the priestly elite and the practices of God-brokering that Jeshu excoriated when he caused a civil disturbance in the Temple. They also experienced the cruel tyranny of the Roman Empire boasting of its Pax Romana. This Roman peace, of course, was not the biblical peace that is the fruit of justice; it was instead the peace that comes by killing or enslaving one's enemies. Within this context Jeshu proclaims service as the model of true authority.

22 For many readers of this gospel, the seven pharisaic damnations signal Christianity's growing anti-Jewishness. Unraveling this text is no easy matter, since elements of these critiques seem consistent with conversations occurring under the umbrella of Judaism. In other words, Jeshu might have said some of these things as a Jew criticizing the religious leadership of his day. When they take on legs, however, and walk outside the Jewish community, and are uttered within the context of a largely Gentile church, they have an entirely different meaning.

23 The section about oaths seems consistent with what we saw earlier in this text when Jeshu repudiated oaths altogether, urging people to speak the simple "yes" or "no" of a community grounded in honesty and trust. Jeshu's critique challenges the bureaucratic mind-set so prevalent among clergy.

24 The inside/outside theme ties together the next two critiques. Obviously it is more important to have the inside than the outside of our dishes clean. Judaism, like all religions, seeks to balance the exoteric (*keva*) and esoteric (*kavanah*) dimensions of practice. The former refers to the regularity of external observance, and the latter points to intentionality, inwardness, and mindfulness. Too much of the former leads to a soulless religious practice; too much of the latter to mere pious sentiment without substance. Truth lies in the balance. Jeshu does not advocate the abandonment of *keva* but its infusion with *kavanah*.

"The greatest among you must always be the one who serves others. For the one who is puffed up with pride will be cut down to size, but the one who is willing to be humble will be made great.[21]

"Damn you,[22] Torah scholars and Pharisees! Pious phonies! You slam the door to God's reign in people's faces. Not only do you not want to go in yourselves, but you won't even let in the people trying to enter.

"Damn you, Torah scholars and Pharisees! Pious phonies! Your proselytizing zeal leads you around the world to convert others, but you end up making them even more damnable than yourselves.

"Damn you, blind leaders! You teach people that oaths aren't binding if they're sworn by the Temple, but they are binding if they're sworn by the Temple's treasury! Blind fools! Which is more important: the treasury or the Temple that makes the treasury holy? You also teach that oaths aren't binding if they're sworn by the altar, but they are binding if they're sworn by the offering on the altar. How blind you are! Which is more important: the offering or the altar that makes the offering holy? Oaths sworn by the altar include all the offerings on it; oaths sworn by the Temple include the God whose house the Temple is; oaths sworn by heaven include both God's throne and the God who reigns from that throne.[23]

"Damn you, Torah scholars and Pharisees! Pious phonies! You're so punctilious in paying your tithes on mint, dill, and cumin, but you ignore what's most important in the Torah: justice, compassion, and trust. The tithing is fine, as long as these more important matters aren't ignored in the process. Blind guides! You strain out the gnat and then gulp down the camel.

"Damn you, Torah scholars and Pharisees! Pious phonies! You scrub the outside of your cup and bowl, but what's inside them are greed and immorality. Blind Pharisees! First clean up what's inside your cup and bowl, then you can clean the outside, too.[24]

(continued on page 185)

25 The capstone criticism drives Jeshu's essential message home with its dramatic image of whitened mausoleums, evident even in contemporary Israel. Behind these gorgeous facades lie only bones and rottenness. So too the veneer of religion can cover corruption and deceit. As the Latin proverb long ago noted, *corruptio optimi pessima:* "the corruption of the best things is the worst kind of corruption." Nothing corrupts so well as religion. Without religion we would lack archives of holiness, our finest art and architecture, and some of the greatest literature produced by humankind. And yet, because of religion, we have also inherited crusades and inquisitions, ecclesiastical embezzlement, and the entire array of churchly corruption.

"Damn you, Torah scholars and Pharisees! Pious phonies! You're like newly painted mausoleums.[25] From the outside they look beautiful, but inside there's nothing but the bones of dead people and pollution. This is just what you're like. You make an appearance of being God-centered, but inside you're phony and far from what the Torah is really about.

"Damn you, Torah scholars and Pharisees! Pious phonies! You build tombs for the prophets and decorate the monuments of holy people. You tell us, 'If we had been alive in those days, we wouldn't have been part of the murder of these prophets.' You're admitting by your own words that you're the children of those who murdered the prophets. Now you're just finishing up what your parents started. You are snakes as well as being the offspring of snakes. How do you expect to escape damnation?"

1 This text reflects the views of Matthew's community in the 80s. The author knows about the destruction of the Second Temple in 70 C.E. as an accomplished fact ("your house will stand empty and desolate"), and he anticipates the return of Jeshu in glory. All responsibility for the world's evils are placed on the unbelieving Jews, and their religious house stands empty. They have a bankrupt religion. This is the harsh voice of Christian exclusivism.

11 □ Warnings about the Future
(Matthew 23:34-25:46)

"It's for this reason that I send you prophets, teachers of wisdom, and Torah scholars. Some of these you kill on crosses; others you whip in your synagogues, chasing them from one town to another. As a result, the responsibility is yours for all the martyrs' blood that's been shed, from the God-centered Abel to Zechariah, Barachiah's son, whom you murdered between the sanctuary and the altar. Believe me when I tell you that the responsibility for all of this will fall on this generation.

"Jerusalem, Jerusalem, you murder prophets and stone those who are sent to you. How many times have I wanted to gather your children together, just as a mother hen gathers her chicks under her wings. But that hasn't been what you wanted. Now your house will stand empty and desolate. For I'm telling you that you won't see me again until you say, 'Blessings on the one who comes in the Lord's name!'"[1]

While Jeshu was leaving the Temple, his disciples called his attention to the buildings in the Temple complex. "So you see all these buildings?" Jeshu said. "Believe me when I tell you that not one stone of them will be left standing."

(continued on page 189)

2 Did Jeshu have anything to say about the future? Yes, he saw something coming as inevitably as a summer storm rolling toward us on a blackened horizon. Jeshu saw his fellow Jews on a twofold collision course with the Roman Empire. On one side were the hawks of his day, the Zealots, whose military attacks on the Romans would lead to the tragic destruction of Temple and city in 70 c.e. On the other side lay the more dangerous spiritual capitulation to Rome embodied by the Sadducees and all those Jews willing to sell their spiritual birthright, Esau-like, for a lentil stew made of Roman perks and privileges. Like all the great prophets of Israel, Jeshu's message was not primarily about the future. It was a call to *teshuvah,* to turning, in the present. If, however, that call was unheeded, then the future would stretch out to its ineluctable consequences. In this context, Jeshu may well have excoriated Jerusalem for its unwillingness to hear the prophetic voice resounding in all of his teachings, and he may have used the beautiful metaphor of God as a mother hen seeking to gather her chicks.

⚛ Certainly Jeshu, like any devout Jew, believed that the world continually being created by God would one day end. In the beautiful image of Isaiah (34:4), God will one day roll up the universe like a scroll. The details of that ending, however, lie beyond anything we can know or about which we should be concerned. We must deal with the smaller endings of our own experience: the death that always lies just a heartbeat away and the death that we experience each night of our existence as we slip from waking into sleeping consciousness. As the Jesuit poet Gerard Manley Hopkins expressed it so succinctly in an untitled poem: "All life death does end and each day dies with sleep."

Jeshu then sat down on the Mount of Olives, where his disciples came to him privately and said, "Let us know when all of this will happen, and tell us what the sign will be of your coming in glory and of the end of this age of the world." "Be on the lookout," he answered, "and don't let anyone fool you. A lot of people will come, claiming to be the Messiah, and many will be taken in by them. You'll hear about wars and rumors of wars, but don't be upset. These things are bound to happen, but it doesn't mean that it's the end. Ethnic groups and nations will struggle with one another for power, and some areas will experience famine and earthquakes. All these things are just the beginning of the suffering that's coming.

"There will be people who will turn you over for punishment, even execution; you'll be hated in every nation because you bear my name. Many will fall by the wayside and end up betraying and hating one another. Many false prophets will appear and lead a lot of people astray. Love will grow cold all over as more and more people neglect the Torah. The only people who are going to make it are those who persevere to the end. The good news of God's reign will be announced all over the world, as a witness to the nations everywhere, before the end comes.

"So when you see what the prophet Daniel called 'the abomination of desolation' standing in the holy place (let the reader note what this means), then everyone in Judea should run for the hills. People in their roof-gardens shouldn't go downstairs and get their valuables; farmers in the field shouldn't stop to grab their shirts. Pity the pregnant women and nursing mothers at this time! Pray that you don't have to do this in the winter or on the Sabbath, because there's going to be suffering at that time such as this universe has never seen from creation until now—and never will see again. If this suffering weren't mitigated, humankind simply wouldn't survive it. But for the sake of those whom God has chosen, the days of suffering will be shortened.[2]

(continued on page 191)

3 These are the concerns of the early community. Once they begin to wait for a figure coming in the clouds, then rumors about that *parousia* or second coming abound, as well as the whole industry of making calendars about the end-times. From that day to our own, large numbers of Christians have missed Jeshu's message about the present moment and have strayed on to this false path of trying to figure out when the end will come. But Jeshu taught that only our heavenly Parent knows about the end. This should be neither our concern nor our focus. What is real for us is the here and now, the present moment with all its possibilities for life and choice, for love and compassion, for service and surrender. If we miss this central thrust of Jeshu's teaching, we miss it all. We are left then with nothing but the empty husks of televangelism.

4 Although Jeshu announced a middle way between rebellion and collaboration, he also saw with great clarity that most of the Jewish leadership would not choose this middle way. Hot-blooded Jewish youth felt that they, David-like, could topple the Goliath of Rome, while the older class of Jewish privilege dreamed of increasing their own affluence and power by selling their souls to the status quo. Jeshu's words find their original setting in this context. The Temple—and indeed the whole Jewish world following one or the other of these two ill-advised paths—was doomed for disaster, a destruction that would occur within the lifetime of Jeshu's contemporaries, within "this present generation."

"At that time, if people say to you, 'Look, here is the Messiah!' or 'There's the Messiah!' don't trust them. For false messiahs and false prophets will be popping up everywhere, and they'll be performing all sorts of signs and wonders to try to deceive those whom God has chosen. Notice that I'm telling you this ahead of time, so if people tell you that there's a messiah in the desert, don't go out there; and if they tell you that there's a messiah hidden away somewhere, don't trust them. For when I come in glory, it will be as visible as the lightning that flashes across the whole sky from east to west. Wherever there's a cadaver, the birds of prey will manage to find it.[3]

"But immediately after the trouble of those times, 'The sun will be darkened, and the moon will fail to shine; the stars will fall from the sky, and the powers of heaven will be shaken.' Then my sign will appear in heaven, and all the tribes of the earth will weep as they see me coming on the clouds of heaven with power and great glory. With the blast of a trumpet I'll send out my angels to the four winds to gather God's chosen from one end of heaven to the other.

"There's something you can learn from the fig tree. When its branches are green and leaves begin to appear, you know that summer is near. In the same way, when you see all these things happen, you'll know that I'm close enough to be on your doorstep. Believe me when I tell you that this present generation[4] will not have passed away until all of these things have taken place. Heaven and earth will pass away, but not my words.

(continued on page 193)

5 If Jeshu was indeed speaking of a coming clash with Rome, then what words of his apply to that disaster? Here we can understand the language of two men working in the field and one being taken while the other is left behind, or two women grinding flour at the mill meeting a similar fate, one killed and one miraculously saved. These are consistent with the earlier comments that admonish people in the roof garden to leave town without stopping to get their valuables and for farmers to flee from the field without reaching for their shirts.

6 The theme of readiness begins to take a central place in Jeshu's teaching. Unfortunately, when Christians shift their attention to end-time dramas, the whole meaning of that readiness changes. Instead of being a readiness in the moment for the in-breaking of God's reign, it now becomes a readiness for an end-time disaster. I recently asked a group of college-age Christians what they thought they were asking for when they prayed "The Kingdom come" in the Lord's Prayer. They all said they were praying for the end of the world. What a tragic misdirection of Christianity's basic message and the power of Jeshu's preaching about the availability of God's Kingdom in the here and now. Christians should pray for the end of their egos, not the end of the world.

"As for the precise schedule for all of this, no one else knows but my heavenly Parent—not the angels in heaven, not even the Son. When I come in glory, it will be just like Noah's time. In those days before the flood, people went on eating and drinking and getting married, right up to the time that Noah went into the ark. Just as they didn't know what was happening until the flood came and washed them away, that's how it will be with people when I come in glory.

"At that time there will be two men working in the field; one will be taken away and one left behind. Two women will be grinding flour at the mill; one will be taken away and one left behind.[5] So be on the lookout, because you don't know precisely when your Lord is coming. You have to realize that if a homeowner knew what time the robber was coming, he would have watched his house and not allowed the robber to break in. That's why you have to be ready all the time, because I may be coming when you least expect me.

"So how does a master decide which of his servants is smart and trustworthy, the kind of person he can put in charge of things, one who will make sure that everything gets done at the right time? That lucky servant will be the one the master finds working hard when he comes home. Believe me when I tell you that the master will make this servant his household supervisor. And how does a master decide which of his servants is worthless? That servant will be the one who, thinking that his master is delayed, starts to beat his fellow servants and party with the heavy drinkers. The master will come home on a day when that servant isn't expecting him and at a time he doesn't know, and then the master will punish him. The master will carve him up and let him share the fate of the pious phonies. That's a place where there will be a lot of weeping and grinding of teeth in despair.[6]

(continued on page 195)

7 The ten young women at the wedding party provide a wonderful picture of the need for readiness and attention, key ingredients in any spiritual practice. Unfortunately, instead of understanding the groom as the perfect teacher in the here and now, a later mind-set turns this story into a parable of the end-time—ironically the very time about which Jeshu has already said that he knows nothing and in which he therefore presumably has no interest at all.

"When that day comes, God's reign will be like ten young women in a wedding party who took their lamps and went to meet the bridegroom. Now five of these young women were foolish, while five were wise. The five foolish ones took their lamps but failed to bring along any extra lamp oil. The five wise ones brought along both lamps and extra oil. Since the groom proved late in coming, the young women began to nod and fall asleep. But in the middle of the night they heard a shout: 'The groom is here; come out to meet him.' All ten woke up and got their lamps ready. At that point, the foolish women said to the wise ones, 'Give us some of your oil, because our lamps are going out.' But they replied, 'There may not be enough for all of us; you'd better go somewhere and buy some.' While the foolish women were away, the groom arrived, and those who were ready went in with him to the wedding reception, and the doors were closed. When the other women arrived later, they asked the groom to open the doors. But the groom answered, 'I honestly don't know who you are.' This is why you have to be on the lookout, because you don't know the groom's schedule.[7]

"Another image of God's reign is the story of a master about to go on a trip who called together his personal servants and put them in charge of some of his money. Judging the differences in their ability to handle money, he gave one the equivalent of ten years' salary, another the equivalent of five years' salary, and a third the equivalent of one year's salary. The one who received the largest amount immediately went out and doubled his money through shrewd financial dealings; the same thing happened with the servant who received the second-largest amount; but the one who received the least money dug a hole in the ground and buried it.

(continued on page 197)

8 The second parable embodies a remarkable truth about the spiritual life. It grows exponentially. So often a young person at the college where I teach makes the simple decision to come to one of the afternoon meditations. The experience of meditation then leads to another decision, perhaps to try the program in yoga or to attend one of the other religious activities available on campus. This leads to a decision to make a meditation retreat or attend a spiritual conference. That student also feels drawn to read certain books, something by the Dalai Lama or Thomas Merton. Doors keep opening doors, and soon the student has embarked on a rich spiritual practice. The original "money" had to be invested; the spiritual market is a bullish one, beyond every dream of Wall Street.

"A long time later the master came home and went over the accounts with the servants. The one who had received the most stepped forward and said, 'Master, I've doubled the money you gave me.' 'Good job!' the master said to him. 'You're an excellent servant and worthy of my trust. Since you've done such a fine job with small matters, I'll give you responsibility for more important things. Come in with me and share my abundance.' The servant who had received the second-largest amount stepped forward and gave the same report of how he had doubled his money. The master responded to him in the same way, inviting him to come in with him and share his abundance. Then the one who had received the least stepped forward and said, 'Master, I know that you're a hard man, reaping where you didn't sow and harvesting fields you never planted. So I was afraid and hid your money in the ground. Here's everything you gave me.' But the master said to him, 'What a poor and worthless servant you are! You know that I reap where I didn't sow and harvest fields I never planted, so you should have deposited all the money in the bank so that I would have received it back with interest when I returned. This money will therefore be taken from you and given to the servant who was entrusted with the most. For even more will be given to the one who has a lot, and even a little will be taken from the one who has next to nothing. Throw this worthless servant outside, where there will be weeping and grinding of teeth.'[8]

(continued on page 199)

9 Although the description of Jeshu as messianic king comes from a later tradition, the essential story seems to summarize perfectly the heart of his teaching. We see here the intimate connections among the three loves enunciated in Jeshu's choice of the cardinal *mitzvot:* the text of Deuteronomy exhorting us to love God with all our being and the text of Leviticus commanding us to love both self and neighbor.

10 The image of final judgment burns brightly in the night sky of Jewish imagination at this period of history. Who will prove to be on God's side in that final day? Will it be those who give their lifeblood opposing the occupation forces of the Empire? Will it be those who live the most Jewishly observant life despite the allurements of the pagan environment? No, Jeshu proclaims; it will be the ones who reach out to those in need, imitating the God who from the beginning proved himself to be a God of the oppressed.

11 Many Christians believe that it is orthodoxy of belief that guarantees and is a sign of salvation. Paul put Christians on this path with his preoccupation with faith. If we say the right words with our lips and have the right belief in our hearts, then we will surely be among the sheep on that last day. But this story points out with inescapable clarity that the separation of sheep and goats is based not on correctness of belief but on the simple practice of meeting God in the needs of the marginalized neighbor. The one who is hungry, thirsty, imprisoned, and unwelcome becomes the sole criterion for the final reckoning. One need not know the name of Jeshu—or anything about Jeshu, for that matter. One only has to know the neighbor in need and respond with compassion for God's heart to be touched and the gates of heaven to swing open.

"When I come in my glory, accompanied by all the angels, I will sit on the royal throne as all the people of the world are gathered before me.**9** And I will divide them into two groups, just as a shepherd divides sheep from goats, putting the sheep on his right side and the goats on his left. At that time, as messianic king,**10** I will say to those on my right, 'Come here, all of you who have been blessed by my heavenly Parent, and inherit the glory that has been prepared for you from creation. For I was hungry and you fed me; I was thirsty and you gave me something to drink. I was a stranger and you made me feel welcome, in need of clothes and you gave them to me, sick and you visited me, in jail and you came to see me.' Then the God-centered people will answer, 'Lord, when did we see you hungry and feed you, or thirsty and give you something to drink? When were you the stranger we welcomed or the person in need of clothes whom we took care of, or the sick person we visited, or the person in jail we came to see?' And I will answer them and say, 'Believe me when I tell you this: if you did any of these things for the least important of my brothers and sisters, you did it for me.'

"Then I will say to those on my left, 'Get away from me; you are damned to eternal fire with the devil and his agents. For I was hungry and you didn't feed me; I was thirsty and you gave me nothing to drink. I was a stranger and you did nothing to make me feel welcome, in need of clothes and you did nothing to help me out, sick and you never visited me, in jail and you never came to see me.' And they will answer, 'Lord, when did we see you in any need and neglect to help you?' But my only answer will be, 'Believe me when I tell you this: if you failed to do any of these things for the person you consider least important, you failed to do it for me.' Now those on my left will be sent off to eternal punishment, but the God-centered people on my right will enter into eternal life."**11**

1 Jeshu's arrest took place around Passover, and some of the Temple personnel—priests and elders—were the likely instigators of the plan to turn him over to the Roman authorities, especially since Pontius Pilate, the chief Roman authority in that part of the Empire, would be in the city for the holiday. The affluent priestly class would certainly be the people most threatened by Jeshu. Their goal of keeping the Temple open led them to cooperate with the Romans in tracking down all insurgents or perceived threats to Roman order. Some of these priests would have little use for a young hasid who had already caused a disturbance in the Temple and was even heard prophesying its destruction within the lifetime of his audience.

⚖ The Pharisees, as much as Matthew enjoys castigating them on every occasion, are strangely absent from this scenario. Perhaps Matthew has sufficient respect for the tradition he has received not to tamper with it in this regard. It is neither the Pharisees nor the Jews who killed Jeshu; it is not even all of the Jewish leaders who killed him, though some of those priestly leaders were probably involved in his arrest. The Roman totalitarian state killed Jeshu, just as it killed thousands of others of his fellow Jews. And the Roman system killed Jeshu because it found him guilty as a political criminal, a freedom fighter, a brigand, a messianic leader—in short, a would-be king.

2 The lovely story of the anointing foretells the normally prescribed ritual that will later be neglected because of the hurry to bury Jeshu before the Sabbath began. The fact that this is one of two places in the gospel narrative where Jeshu explicitly refers to something being done "in memory of" (the other, of course, being the bread and wine ritual) has undoubted significance. Sadly—and this is surely reflective of the position of women at this time—the name of the woman is not remembered, though Jeshu's response suggests that we are at the site of a memorable event in his life. Later tradition will identify her with the Mary called Magdalene, but there is no textual support for this claim.

12 □ The Path from Death to Life
(Matthew 26:1-28:20)

When Jeshu had finished these teachings, he said to his disciples, "You know that Pesach is just two days away, and it is then that I will be handed over to be crucified." It was at this same time that the chief priests and the elders of the people[1] gathered together in the palace of Kayafa, the high priest, where they plotted to arrest Jeshu secretly and kill him. But they said, "We can't do this at the time of the high holiday, or the people will riot."

When Jeshu was in Beit-anyah, at the home of Shimon the leper, a woman approached him with an alabaster jar filled with expensive perfume, and while he was sitting there at table she poured it on his head. Now when the disciples saw this, they were upset and said, "What a waste! That perfume could have been sold for a lot of money, which could then have been given to the poor." Jeshu was aware of their criticism, and he said to them, "Why do you bother this woman? She's done something very beautiful for me. There will always be poor people around who need your generosity, but I won't always be around. In pouring this perfume on me, she was preparing my body for burial. Believe me when I tell you that wherever in the world this good news is proclaimed, what this woman has done will be told in her memory."[2]

(continued on page 203)

△ Time and again Jeshu loves and praises the spontaneity of true faith, so different from the encrusted response of a cautious piety. This is a moment that deserves to be recounted; this is a story that should be told again and again. And why? In memory of her. Who is she? A nameless woman who stepped boldly across the boundaries of her world and accomplished a perfect deed. We sense the shock of the men, both Jeshu's disciples and Shimon's other guests, at this woman acting so "out of place." They undoubtedly drew their robes close to their bodies as she passed lest they be stained with her female contagion. Only Jeshu remained calm, seeing the deeper reality unfold, immune to the societal constraints of his peers. She was indeed doing a beautiful thing, a generous act, and only one man in the crowd knew that. In defending her from the carping criticisms of the men, Jeshu defended all women everywhere from the male bias that continues to misperceive, misjudge, and devalue the generosity and beauty of the feminine.

3 Was there someone called Judah among Jeshu's close circle of disciples? The discrepancies in the various lists of the twelve lead us to surmise that it was more important to state that there were twelve than it was to know who they were. In other words, the symbolism of twelve apostles, like twelve tribes, soon became central to the Christian story. Several names on the differing lists may be in doubt and none with greater significance for our story than Judah. Judah became the primary figure to embody the virulent anti-Jewishness that comes to characterize Christian polemic. Is it merely a coincidence that his very name means "the Jew"? Is "the Jew" from Jeshu's most intimate circle of disciples who betrays his master part of a Christian midrash to heighten and highlight the larger fiction of a Jewish plot to kill Jeshu?

Why invent a Jewish plot in the first place? It is both part of an increasing anti-Jewish polemic as well as a consequence of whitewashing and downplaying the Roman involvement in Jeshu's death. After all, Jeshu's execution as a felon charged with political crimes would hardly open doors to the minds and hearts of Roman citizens. A new political or religious organization, boasting that its founder died in the

(continued on page 204)

Then one of the twelve, the one called Judah from Kriot,[3] went to the chief priests and said, "What are you willing to give me if I turn this Jeshu over to you?" They agreed to pay him thirty silver coins. And from that point on Judah started looking for a good opportunity to betray Jeshu.

(continued on page 205)

electric chair as a convicted criminal, would not readily invite an enthusiastic response from the American public. So Jeshu's story was more and more being told with a spin that exonerated the Romans. Like a seesaw, however, pushing the Romans up necessarily pushed the Jews down. Consequently, Jews began to play an increasingly more important role in these events of the last days of Jeshu's life.

4 In a city teeming with pilgrims for the high holiday, it would not be easy for a group of homeless men from the Galilee to find a place to celebrate the seder, the meal of the first night of Passover in which the story of the Exodus is told. The gospel story provides a fairy-tale kind of scene in which a total stranger offers a space for the holiday dinner. I would rather imagine that Jeshu had some followers in Jerusalem and that one of these disciples provided the needed space.

5 At the meal itself, Jeshu describes the bread as his body to be eaten and the wine as his covenant blood to be drunk. Given Jewish sensitivity about any connection between blood and eating, there is simply no way that Jeshu could have said anything about his disciples eating his body or drinking his blood. But it is entirely possible that Jeshu, thinking ahead to his imminent arrest and execution, compared his body to bread that was broken and his blood to wine that was poured out. And he asked them to remember him when they met again to eat and drink after his death. His vulnerability, after all, was central to his message; his brokenness was crucial to his ability to feed others through his teachings.

Jeshu's disciples came to him to ask about the first day of the holiday, the first day when the matzah is eaten. They wanted to know where he wanted them to prepare the seder. Jeshu told them to go to a certain man in the city and tell him that their teacher said that the appointed time was at hand and that he wanted to celebrate Pesach with his disciples at this man's house.[4] The disciples did what Jeshu told them to do and prepared the seder.

When it was evening, Jeshu took his place at the table with his disciples. And during the meal he said to them, "Believe me when I tell you that one of you will betray me." The disciples were very upset and began to ask, one after the other, "You don't mean me, do you, Lord?" Jeshu responded by saying, "One who has dipped his matzah in the dish with me will betray me. It's true that I must leave you, just as it's written in the scriptures, but my betrayer is nonetheless damned. That man would be better off if he had never been born." It was at this point that the traitor Judah asked him, "You don't mean me, do you, rabbi?" And Jeshu said to him, "Those are your words."

After they resumed eating, Jeshu took some matzah, blessed it, broke it, and gave it to his disciples, saying, "Take this and eat it; this is my body." He also took a cup of wine, blessed it, and gave it to them, saying, "Drink from this, all of you; for this is my blood of the covenant, blood poured out for many, so that the sins of many will be forgiven. I'm telling you now that I will not drink the fruit of the vine again until I drink new wine with you where my heavenly Parent reigns."[5]

(*continued on page* 207)

6 This passage may well be midrash, a sermonic and meditative reconstruction of the events of that last evening, since obviously there were no eye- or ear-witnesses to what Jeshu said in prayer while the disciples were sleeping. It would nevertheless be true that Jeshu was not looking forward to the fate that almost certainly awaited him. If we invest the Temple incident with any kind of historical veracity, then it was a simple matter of waiting for the other shoe to fall to expect his arrest and punishment. So the spirit of this passage, if not the letter, seems accurate. Jeshu's hesitancy in the face of his imminent arrest and execution contradicts the later idea that his primary intention all along was to offer himself as a sacrifice for sin and an appeasement of his heavenly Parent's wrath. Why would he be hesitant if the goal of his whole life was finally at hand?

⚭ This passage, whether it is a reconstruction of the early community or the remembrance of some of the things Jeshu really did and said the night of his arrest, offers a model of Christian prayer, especially in its intercessory form. Prayers of praise and thanks are self-explanatory and need little to justify them, other than the impulses of the human heart in response to the Divine. But there is always something a bit complicated about intercessory prayer. It is natural enough to tell God what we would like to happen to others and to ourselves, but do we really have sufficient knowledge to be sure that our plans are the best ones? There is, after all, an entire genre of stories about people who are granted a wish and end up courting disaster—for example, poor Midas turning his daughter to gold. So the final corrective in this prayer attributed to Jeshu seems instructive: "It's not my will that counts here, but Yours."

After singing a hymn, they went out to the Mount of Olives. Then Jeshu said to them, "This very night you will all take offense at what I must do. As the scriptures tell us, 'I will slay the shepherd, and the sheep of the flock will be scattered.' But after I am raised up, I will go ahead of you to the Galilee." At this point, Rock responded, "Even if it's true that all the others take offense at what you must do, that will never be true of me." Jeshu said to him, "Believe me when I tell you that this very night, before the roosters crow to announce the dawn, you will deny me three times." Rock responded, "Even if I have to die with you, I won't deny you." And all the others said the same thing.

Then Jeshu went with his disciples to a place called Gethsemane, and he said to them, "Stay here while I go over there and pray." Taking Rock and Zebedee's two sons with him, Jeshu was plunged into grief and anguish. "I'm sick to death with the sadness that fills my heart," he said to them, "stay here and keep me company." Going on a little farther, he threw himself face down on the ground and prayed, "My heavenly Parent, if it's possible, let this cup pass me by; and yet, it's not my will that counts here, but yours." Returning to the three disciples and finding them sleeping, Jeshu said to Rock, "Weren't you strong enough to stay awake one hour with me? Stay alert and pray that you won't fall when you're tempted. I know that your heart is in the right place, but your human nature is weak."

Jeshu went back a second time to pray: "My heavenly Parent, if it's not possible for this cup to pass me by without my drinking from it, then I want your will to be done."[6] He returned a second time to his disciples and found them asleep again; they just couldn't keep their eyes open. So he left them again and prayed a third time, using the same words. Then he came back to the disciples and said, "It's just as well you're sleeping now and getting some rest. The appointed time is very close for me to be turned over to sinners. Get up! Let's go! My betrayer is very close."

(continued on page 209)

7 The arrest scene is dramatic and may contain some historical remembrances. After all, there were probably people present at the arrest who were alive to tell the story later on. Perhaps there was a traitor who came with the arresting squad of soldiers. One of the disciples may even have drawn a knife in a futile attempt to stop the arrest. There must have been a good deal of confusion and pandemonium in the event. It makes sense that Jeshu was arrested by the private bodyguard of the high priest and taken to the high priest's house that evening, there to spend the night before being taken to Pilate in the morning. Undoubtedly there would have been an interrogation session at the high priest's house that night.

While Jeshu was still speaking, Judah, one of the twelve, arrived with a large crowd armed with swords and clubs; these were people sent by the chief priests and elders of the people. The traitor had arranged to give them a signal: "The man I kiss is the one you want; arrest him." Immediately Judah went up to Jeshu and said, "Hello, rabbi!" and kissed him. Jeshu said to him, "My friend, this is what you're here for." And with that, the crowd took hold of Jeshu and arrested him.

Suddenly, one of Jeshu's disciples went for his sword and cut off the ear of a servant of the high priest. Jeshu said to the disciple, "Put your sword back where it came from; people who rely on swords die on swords. Don't you know that I can call on my heavenly Parent for help to send instantly more than twelve armies of angels? But how would that fulfill the scriptures that tell us it must happen this way?"

At the same time, Jeshu said to the crowd, "Did you have to come for me with swords and clubs, as though I were an outlaw? I've been sitting in the Temple courtyard day after day teaching there, and no one arrested me. But this whole thing is happening to fulfill the writings of the prophets." At this point, all the disciples deserted him and ran away.[7]

Those who had arrested Jeshu led him off to the house of Kayafa, the high priest, where the Torah scholars and elders had assembled. Rock followed from a distance, as far as the courtyard of the high priest's house; he went inside and sat down with the guards to see how it would all end.

(continued on page 211)

8 This scene in the presence of the high priest presents us with a highly instructive piece of midrash. With no witnesses from Jeshu's disciples around, we would be hard-pressed to imagine this event as containing any historical memories. But a witness testifying that Jeshu had said something about the Temple being destroyed seems credible, especially since Jeshu had indeed prophesied the destruction of the Temple. The charge, of course, would not be blasphemy, as this text suggests, but treason. The Christian community, however, could not conceive Jeshu's trial involving anything but religious issues. And yet the gospel record testifies that the charge on the cross was not "blasphemer" but "King of the Jews."

9 The bulk of this story is a product of Christian meditation on those final fateful events. His followers believed that Jeshu must have been judged as a blasphemer by the entire Sanhedrin (i.e., representatives of all the Jews). They imagined that the Jewish leaders would have been cruel to Jeshu, since Jewish leadership seemed cruel to the Christians in the 80s. They surmised that Jeshu certainly would not have passed up such an opportunity to address the official ruling body of the Jews as to his future role as the central figure in the *parousia,* a glorious returning Messiah. This, at least, was how Christians wanted to remember it, despite the likelihood that nothing like this really happened.

10 Loyalty is tested when a leader is arrested. It seems natural that most of Jeshu's disciples would flee. But Rock goes one step farther down that road. In failing to flee with the others, he puts himself in a position of even greater peril. And now, as Jeshu had prophesied at the Last Supper, he denies his beloved master three times before the rooster announces the morning sunrise. But unlike Judah, who we will shortly see kill himself in despair, Rock weeps bitterly, admitting his failure but still trusting in divine forgiveness.

Certainly there were backsliders and Christian apostates in Matthew's world, and it was consoling to remember that Rock himself, one of the chief apostles, failed in that moment of testing too.

(continued on page 212)

The chief priests and the whole Sanhedrin were looking for some false evidence against Jeshu so that they could have him executed, but they weren't finding much, even though a lot of people were coming forward to give false evidence. Finally, two witnesses came forward who testified, "This man said that he could tear down the Temple of God and rebuild it again in three days." So the high priest stood up and said to Jeshu, "No answers? What about these testimonies against you?" But Jeshu remained silent.[8] Again the high priest addressed him: "I'm putting you under oath. By the living God, tell us whether or not you're the Messiah, God's Son." "Those are your words," Jeshu said to him. "But I will tell you this: any time now you'll see me sitting at the right hand of God's power and coming on the clouds of heaven."[9]

At that point, the high priest tore his robes and said, "Blasphemy! Do we still need any witnesses? How does this whole situation seem to you, now that you've heard him blaspheme with your own ears?" They all answered, "He deserves the death penalty." Then they all began to spit in his face and beat him, while some slapped him, saying, "Show us your prophetic powers, Messiah—who's hitting you this time?"

Meanwhile, Rock was sitting outside in the courtyard when one of the serving girls came up to him and said, "You too were with this Jeshu from the Galilee." But in front of everyone, Rock denied it and said, "I don't know what you're talking about." Then he went out on the porch, where another serving girl saw him and said to the people standing around, "This man was with Jeshu of Nazareth." Again Rock denied knowing Jeshu, this time with an oath. After a little while, the people standing around came up to Rock and said, "Honestly, now, you've got to be one of them; even your accent gives you away." Then Rock began to curse and swear that he didn't know Jeshu—and just then the rooster crowed. Rock remembered what Jeshu had said—that he would deny him three times before the rooster crowed—and Rock left the courtyard, weeping bitterly.[10]

(continued on page 213)

Perseverance in persecution was becoming a popular theme in Christian writings of the first century and will remain a relevant matter until almost three hundred years later, when the Edict of Toleration issued by the Emperor Constantine will finally make Christianity a *religio licita* (a legal association) in the Roman Empire.

11 Our text now describes the movement from the high priest's house to the Antonium, Pilate's base of operations during high holidays. Roman business was handled early in the day, and Jeshu was undoubtedly added to a few other political prisoners who were to be crucified and buried before Passover began that evening at sunset. This is the bare historical framework, and it seems reliable. Any details beyond the facts that Jeshu was judged by the governor, Pontius Pilate, and then crucified and buried probably stem from Christian midrash.

12 This section presents us with three important figures to examine: Judah, Bar-Abba, and Pilate. We discussed Judah earlier and are informed in this section about the circumstances of his death. The connection with the name of a particular place seems fanciful, except as a midrash on the Jeremiah quote. The whole story lacks credibility. Nonetheless, the figure of Judah/Judas continues to fascinate us, even though his reality may lie more in midrash than in history.

At daybreak, all the chief priests and elders of the people met to plan Jeshu's execution. Putting him in chains, they led him off and handed him over to Pilate, the governor.[11]

When Judah, who had betrayed Jeshu, saw that he had been condemned, he had a change of heart. He returned the thirty silver coins to the chief priests and the elders and told them, "I've sinned in betraying an innocent man." "What does that have to do with us?" they answered. "That's your business." Throwing the coins into the sanctuary, Judah left them; then he went out and hanged himself.

The chief priests picked up the silver coins and said, "Since this is blood money, we're not permitted to put it into the Temple treasury." So they agreed to use the money to buy Potter's Field as a cemetery for foreigners. And that's why, even today, you can hear people call that area "Blood Field." All of this fulfilled the oracle of the prophet Jeremiah: "And they took the thirty silver coins, the amount the people of Israel had agreed to pay for him, and used the money to buy the Potter's Field, just as the Lord commanded me."[12]

Jeshu, meanwhile, was brought before the governor, who asked him, "Are you the King of the Jews?" "Those are your words," answered Jeshu. But when he was accused by the chief priests and the elders, Jeshu made no response. So Pilate said to him, "Don't you hear all these charges they're bringing against you?" But much to the surprise of the governor, Jeshu didn't say a single word in his own defense.

(continued on page 215)

13 The second figure, Bar-Abba (Barabbas), is even less likely to have been real. His name in Aramaic means "Son of the Father," and in some texts his first name is Jeshu. He clearly seems to be a creation of Christian imagination, since the perpetrator of the political crime that has been disconnected from Jeshu (who has become a religious martyr) needs to be pinned on someone. Bar-Abba serves as a magnet drawing to himself all the political realities of Jeshu's execution. This leaves us with Jeshu as a religious prisoner—indeed, a martyr—untainted by any political scandal. The difficulty with the story, of course, is that it is probably not true.

⚠ The very idea of a Roman leader releasing a political criminal in a city crowded with visitors seems bizarre, if not downright ridiculous. However unimaginative the Romans were in their rule, they were not dumb. And when we further remember that Pilate probably had some inkling of the holiday being celebrated, a Jewish festival of freedom commemorating how their God had delivered them from the oppressive tyranny of the Pharaoh, then there is even less likelihood of such an incendiary action. Even a literal-minded Roman could figure out that the Emperor probably seemed a lot like the Pharaoh in the Jewish imagination.

14 Finally we come to the figure of Pilate, a governor of such insensitivity and cruelty that even the Romans (who were well able to tolerate cruelty in their procurators) pulled him out of office for his criminal behavior. Why, then, these touching stories of a wife moved by a dream and a tyrant washing his hands of a crime? Clearly for the reasons we stated earlier. The attempt to tell the story in such a way as to exonerate the Romans is pulling Matthew into the great lie that the Jews, not the Roman imperial system, killed Jeshu. And as part of this propaganda, Matthew pens the line that would damn him forever if he had any idea of the evil it would perpetrate in history. The Jews cry out that the blood of Jeshu should be on them and on their children. Here are words strong enough to fuel pogroms and persecutions for centuries.

It was the governor's custom to release a prisoner—anyone the crowd asked for—at the time of the high holiday. There was a notorious prisoner in jail at that time, a man named Jeshu Bar-Abba.[13] So when the crowd was gathered together, Pilate asked them, "Do you want me to release for you Jeshu Bar-Abba or Jeshu who is called the Messiah?" Pilate[14] asked this, knowing full well that the chief priests and elders had arrested Jeshu out of spite. While Pilate was sitting there as judge, his wife sent him a message: "Have nothing to do with that God-centered man; I had a disturbing dream last night about him." Meanwhile, the chief priests and the elders persuaded the crowd to ask Pilate to free Bar-Abba and have Jeshu put to death. "Which of these two men do you want me to release for you?" asked the governor. And they answered, "Bar-Abba." Pilate then asked them, "So what shall I do with this Jeshu who is called the Messiah?" They all said, "Crucify him." But Pilate asked, "What crime has he committed?" But they shouted all the more, "Crucify him."

(continued on page 217)

15 Some like to argue that the gospels are antipharisaic, perhaps even anti-Jewish, but definitely not anti-Semitic. Such unfortunately is not the case. The calling-down of a curse that would be part of the blood legacy of Jews for the rest of human history, whether they converted to Christianity or not, is certainly an attack on the Jewish people that can be called nothing less than anti-Semitic. Even someone as insensitive to anti-Semitism as Mel Gibson agreed to delete the subtitles from the scene in his movie *The Passion of the Christ* where the Jewish crowd calls this curse upon themselves.

16 The word often translated as "thief" does not refer to a household thief but a brigand, one who resisted the Romans by every means possible. In our terms, such a person could be called a freedom fighter.

When Pilate saw that his efforts were useless and that there were even signs of a possible riot, he took some water, washed his hands in front of everyone, and said, "I'm innocent of this man's blood; he's your responsibility." Then all the people answered, "Let his blood be on us and on our children."**15** Then Pilate released Bar-Abba for them and ordered Jeshu to be whipped and handed over for execution.

After this, the governor's soldiers took Jeshu into the Roman headquarters, where the whole battalion gathered around him. Stripping him, they covered him with a military cloak. Then they put on his head a crown they had woven out of thorns and put a reed in his hand. They mocked him by kneeling in front of him and saying, "We salute you, King of the Jews!" They spat on him and took the reed from his hand and beat him over the head with it. When they had finished their games with him, they stripped him of the military cloak, dressed him again in his own clothes, and led him away to crucify him.

As they were leaving they met a man from Cyrene named Shimon, and they forced him to carry Jeshu's cross. When they came to the place called Gulgolta (which means "place of the skull"), they offered him wine to drink, mixed with gall; but when he tasted it, he wouldn't drink it. After that, they crucified him and threw dice for his clothes. Then they sat down at the cross to guard him, after they had posted over his head a notice of his crime: "This is Jeshu, the King of the Jews."

Two freedom fighters**16** were crucified with Jeshu, one on his right and one on his left. People passing by shouted insults at Jeshu, shaking their heads and saying, "So this is the one who can destroy the Temple and rebuild it in three days. You'd better learn how to save yourself. If you're God's son, get yourself down from that cross."

(continued on page 219)

17 Several of these imaginative inventions play a role in developing Matthew's story of Jewish malevolence. Threads of Jewishness and anti-Jewishness weave crazily through the quilt of Matthew's narrative. The Jewishness reflects the stratum connected with the hidden gospel; the anti-Jewishness comes from Matthew's community in its tensions with the rise of rabbinic Judaism. It is completely possible that Jeshu, as a devout Jew, prayed Psalm 22 on the cross. It begins with the words Matthew puts in Jeshu's mouth: "My God, my God, why have you forsaken me?" And yet, this is by no means a cry of final despair, for the same psalm goes on to say, "In you our ancestors trusted; they trusted, and you delivered them." It was surely with trust in the same God who had been with him all his life that Jeshu cried out a last time before expiring on the cross.

18 What we have here seems mostly midrash. The whole story about the empty tomb in Matthew's community, a story that motivates a series of counterstories among the rabbinic Jews of his time, is retrojected into the events of 30 c.e. Most of the events described here are prophecies historicized. After all, we are again without witnesses; even the women are standing at a distance at the time of the crucifixion. Matthew plays a fairly open hand here, giving us the text that leads to each "event" described. The story moves quickly to fanciful ideas of the Temple's veil being torn in two (something we suspect Josephus would have mentioned had it literally happened), spirits roaming the streets, and bizarre weather patterns.

19 It defies credibility to deal with these items as real events. The folks waking up in the tombs, for example, apparently had to hang around in the graveyards until after Jeshu's resurrection: from Friday afternoon until Sunday morning. This is because the developing Christian story includes the "harrowing of hell"—Jeshu descending to the nether regions and releasing the souls of the righteous that had been waiting there since heaven's gates were closed by Adam's sin. So Matthew's narrative, if understood in a literal sense, falters on the timing. The risen souls are awakened to life at the time of Jeshu's death, but they can't

(continued on page 220)

The chief priests, along with the Torah scholars and elders, behaved the same way, jeering at him and saying, "He saved others, but it looks as if he can't save himself. If he's the King of Israel, we'd like to see him come down right now from that cross; then we'd trust him. He relied on God, so let God rescue him if God really wants to. After all, he claimed to be God's son." Even the freedom fighters who were crucified with him were mocking him in the same way.

The whole area was covered with darkness from noon until three o'clock. It was about then that Jeshu screamed out loudly, *"Eli! Eli! Lama shevaktani?"* This means, "My God! My God! Why have you abandoned me?"**17** When some of those standing around heard this, they said, "This man is calling out to Elijah." One of them immediately ran up, took a sponge, soaked it with vinegar, and, putting it on a stick, gave it to Jeshu to drink. But the rest of them said, "Wait a minute and let's see if Elijah comes to save him." But at that point, Jeshu let out another loud scream and died.

At that very moment, the curtain in the Temple was ripped in two from top to bottom.**18** The earth quaked; rocks split apart; graves were opened; and the bodies of many of the saints who had died were raised to life. After Jeshu's resurrection, they left their tombs and went into the holy city, where they appeared to many people.**19** When the Roman officer and the soldiers who were on duty with him experienced the earthquake and all the things that were happening, they were terrified and said, "This really must have been God's son!"

Now there were many women there who were looking on from a distance; these were women who had followed Jeshu from the Galilee, looking after his needs. Among them were Miriam from Magdala, Miriam the mother of Jacob and Josef, and the mother of Zebedee's sons.

(continued on page 221)

really function until Jeshu has released them at the time of his resurrection.

⚠ In light of the three-leveled universe in which people lived at this time, all these stages in Jeshu's career constitute his journey through those levels. His existence with the Father from all eternity shows us the beginning of the journey, when he is still at home in heaven with God. His birth brings him down to the earth plane. His death takes him into the underworld, where he releases the spirits of the righteous who have been waiting there. His resurrection brings him back to the earth plane, just as his ascension takes him back to the heaven plane where his journey began. As a theological construct, this journey has significance. Trying to chart it as though it were a trip from Chicago to Peoria and back again leads to the mental bankruptcy of fundamentalism.

20 The Romans crucified thousands of Jews in the first century c.e. And yet, to this date, archaeologists have found only one corpse of a man who was crucified. Why this lack of bodies? Because part of the humiliation of crucifixion was to dump the bodies in ditches, denying them proper burial rites. This was probably the fate of Jeshu's body as well. All the rest is midrash, including Josef and the rock tomb, the seal and the sentinels.

That same evening, there appeared a rich man from Ramatayim named Josef; he was a disciple of Jeshu. He approached Pilate, asking for Jeshu's corpse; Pilate agreed and gave an order that the corpse be turned over to this Josef. Taking the corpse, Josef wrapped it in a clean linen sheet, and placed it in his own new tomb, just cut out of the rock. Then he rolled a large stone across the entrance to the tomb and left. Miriam of Magdala and the other Miriam stayed behind, sitting facing the tomb.[20]

On the next day—the day after the day of preparation for Pesach— the chief priests and the Pharisees met with Pilate and said, "Sir, we remember that while that impostor was alive, he claimed that he would be raised to life again after three days. Give orders, therefore, that the tomb be secured until the third day, so that his disciples don't come and steal the corpse and then tell everybody that he's raised from the dead. A last deceit of this sort would be worse than any earlier one." Pilate said to them, "You have guards; go ahead and make the tomb as secure as you know how." So they left and secured the tomb by putting a seal on the stone and placing a guard on duty.

After the Sabbath had ended, toward dawn of that Sunday, Miriam of Magdala and the other Miriam went to see the tomb. Suddenly they felt the earth quake, for an angel of the Lord had descended from heaven, had rolled back the stone, and was sitting on it. His presence was dazzling, like a bolt of lightning, and his clothes were as white as snow. The guards were so shocked, they were paralyzed with fear. The angel said to the women, "Don't be afraid; I know that you're looking for Jeshu, who was crucified. He's not here. He has been raised from the dead, just as he told you he would be. Come here and see the place where he was laid out. Then hurry and tell his disciples that he's been raised from the dead and will be going ahead of them to the Galilee, where he'll meet them. That's my message to you."

(continued on page 223)

21 This is one of the most intriguing lines in the gospel. In this line, Matthew steps out of the role of narrator of events in the 20s and speaks to us for a brief moment from his own life-world in the 80s or 90s. The Jews are spreading stories around "today"; so too, of course, are the Christians. It is precisely the polemical exchange of these stories that provides the context for this part of the narrative.

Some Christians by the time of Matthew were talking about an empty tomb as a sign of Jeshu's resurrection. Since this story appears nowhere in the letters of Paul, written in the 50s, it is probably of later vintage. The rabbinic Jews quite logically responded to this story by asserting that an empty tomb proves nothing, since the body could have been stolen. The Christians then developed a counterstory that the tomb had been guarded. The Jews then asked why the guards did not see the resurrection and testify to it. The Christians responded that the guards were bribed by the priests not to repeat what they saw. At this point, the whole story and counterstory polemic seems ludicrous. Could any priests really be evil enough to fight the evidence of a physical resurrection? Could guards actually be bribed by a few coins to keep silent about what would have been the most momentous event in human history, a dead body now alive once again emerging from a tomb? What we have here is clearly not history but low-level polemics.

⚿ What did happen that Sunday morning? Probably nothing in the physical world, nothing that a video camera could have caught for the early-morning breaking news. And yet, a great deal happened in the lives and hearts of some of Jeshu's followers. Individually, and occasionally in pairs or larger groups, they had profoundly transformative religious experiences. Their lives were stretched to previously unknown dimensions, and they knew that Jeshu was alive and would continue to reign in their hearts as Lord. This transformative miracle continues to this day and lies at the core of all Christian mysticism. The tomb empty of a human body at the end of this gospel is the midrashic partner of the womb empty of human seed at its beginning. Both point to the infinite power of the divine reality, a power that can change death to life.

Filled with a mixture of fear and joy, the women quickly ran from the tomb to bring the news to Jeshu's disciples. Suddenly, Jeshu himself met them and said, "Greetings!" The women approached him and fell at his feet in adoration. Then Jeshu said to them, "Don't be afraid. Go and tell my brothers to go to the Galilee, where they'll see me."

While the women were on their way, some of the guards went back to the city to tell the chief priests everything that had happened. The chief priests met with the elders and made plans to bribe the guards and instruct them to tell everybody that Jeshu's disciples had come during the night and stolen the corpse while they were sleeping. They also told the guards that if the governor got wind of the matter, they would take care of him, and the guards would have nothing to worry about. So the guards took the bribe and did what they were told, and this is the story the Jews are still spreading around today.[21]

(continued on page 227)

22 The final mandate of Jeshu, the words we know as the "great commission," are clearly the words of Matthew's community. It is inconceivable that the historical Jeshu would instruct his disciples with the proto-trinitarian formula used for baptism in the early community. But Christians have nonetheless used these words to spread their version of the gospel to the nations of the world. A new religion, especially one that has so often been viciously exclusivist, was hardly what Jeshu had in mind. The persecutions and pogroms, the inquisitions and religious wars, the arrogant proselytizing in his name, the defamation of other paths of holiness—none of this was what he intended. The religion that bears his name is being called to a profound conversion at this time: a conversion to God and an embracing of the many ways to the center of reality that other human beings are walking in justice and in compassion. Never have humility and a willingness to engage in interreligious dialogue been more desperately needed.

Jeshu called people to a spiritual consciousness that transcended religious affiliation and all the boundaries of society based on gender, wealth, or social status. He reminded people that religions are vehicles *to* the Divine and not containers *of* the Divine. He demonstrated the compassion we all should show for our fellow travelers in this journey of life, challenging us to see that everything in its deepest reality is God, and that nothing can ever be separate from God. His commandments are to surrender ourselves totally to God and to manifest that surrender through lives based on justice in the pursuit of peace. We are to love God with all our heart, soul, and mind; and we are to love our neighbor as ourselves. We are called to have the courage to take up the difficulties of our lives, the crosses placed in all our paths, and to follow his example of love and forgiveness. We are invited to be open to the reign of God that embraces us in every present moment.

The eleven disciples went to the hill in the Galilee where Jeshu had told them to go. When they saw him, they fell down at his feet, though some of them held back. Jeshu came close to them and talked with them. "I have been given all authority in heaven and on earth. Go and make disciples from every people, immersing them in the name of the Father, the Son, and the Holy Spirit.[22] Teach them to obey everything that I've commanded you.

(continued on page 227)

23 The Jeshu whose name the angel said would be Immanuel, "God with Us," tells us in the closing lines of this gospel that he will indeed always be with us, always be Immanuel. And the new Torah ("everything that I've commanded you") will reach every human heart—not, of course, in the sense that everyone should become a Christian. What Jeshu was talking about can never be achieved by the mere replacement of one religion with another. The words of Jeshu are heard whenever a heart opens to the divine reality, whether that heart be the heart of a Jew, a Muslim, a Buddhist, or yes, even a Christian. This is the mystic core of Jeshu's message, the hidden gospel of Matthew that we have been pursuing in these pages. For Jeshu did not preach religion but reality, and no one religion has a corner on reality. Humanity will never meet in a common religion; it can meet, however, in a common reality: the consciousness of our divine nature and the realization that we can indeed live in peace.

And remember that I'm always with you, right up to the day when this present world order ends."**23**

Suggested Readings ☐

Albright, W. F., and C. S. Mann, eds. *The Anchor Bible: Matthew.* Garden City, N.Y.: Doubleday, 1971.

Borg, Marcus J. *The Heart of Christianity: Rediscovering a Life of Faith.* San Francisco: HarperSanFrancisco, 2003.

———. *Jesus, a New Vision: Spirit, Culture, and the Life of Discipleship.* San Francisco: Harper & Row, 1987.

———, ed. *The Lost Gospel Q: The Original Sayings of Jesus.* Berkeley, Calif.: Seastone/Ulysses Press, 1996.

———. *Meeting Jesus Again for the First Time: The Historical Jesus and the Heart of Contemporary Faith.* San Francisco: HarperSanFrancisco, 1994.

———. *Reading the Bible Again for the First Time: Taking the Bible Seriously but Not Literally.* San Francisco: HarperSanFrancisco, 2001.

Cameron, Ron, ed. *The Other Gospels: Non-Canonical Gospel Texts.* Philadelphia: Westminster Press, 1982.

Carroll, James. *Constantine's Sword: The Church and the Jews.* Boston: Houghton Mifflin, 2001.

Crossan, John Dominic. *The Historical Jesus: The Life of a Mediterranean Jewish Peasant.* San Francisco: HarperSanFrancisco, 1991.

———. *Jesus: A Revolutionary Biography.* San Francisco: HarperSanFrancisco, 1994.

Crossan, John Dominic, and Jonathan L. Reed. *Excavating Jesus: Beneath the Stones, Behind the Texts.* San Francisco: HarperSanFrancisco, 2001.

Davies, Stevan, trans. and ed. *The Gospel of Thomas: Annotated and Explained.* Woodstock, Vt.: SkyLight Paths, 2002.

Fiorenza, Elisabeth Schüssler. *In Memory of Her: A Feminist Theological Reconstruction of Christian Origins.* New York: Crossroad, 1985.

Horsley, Richard A., and John S. Hanson. *Bandits, Prophets, and Messiahs: Popular Movements in the Time of Jesus.* San Francisco: Harper & Row, 1988.

Maccoby, Hyam. *Revolution in Judaea: Jesus and the Jewish Resistance.* New York: Taplinger, 1973.

———. *The Sacred Executioner: Human Sacrifice and the Legacy of Guilt.* London: Thames & Hudson, 1982.

Miller, Ron. *The Gospel of Thomas: A Guidebook for Spiritual Practice.* Woodstock, Vt.: SkyLight Paths, 2004.

———. *Wisdom of the Carpenter: 365 Prayers and Meditations of Jesus from the Gospel of Thomas, Lost Gospel Q, Secret Book of James, and the New Testament.* Berkeley, Calif.: Seastone/Ulysses Press, 2002.

Mitchell, Stephen. *The Gospel According to Jesus: A New Translation and Guide to His Essential Teachings for Believers and Unbelievers.* New York: HarperCollins, 1991.

Saldarini, Anthony J. *Matthew's Christian-Jewish Community.* Chicago: University of Chicago Press, 1994.

———. *Pharisees, Scribes, and Sadducees in Palestinian Society: A Sociological Approach.* Wilmington, Del.: Michael Glazier, 1988.

Schaberg, Jane. *The Illegitimacy of Jesus: A Feminist Interpretation of the Infancy Narratives.* San Francisco: Harper & Row, 1987.

Sigal, Phillip. *The Halakah of Jesus of Nazareth According to the Gospel of Matthew.* Lanham, Md.: University Press of America, 1986.

Smallwood, E. Mary. *The Jews under Roman Rule: From Pompey to Diocletian.* Leiden, The Netherlands: E. J. Brill, 1981.

Spong, John Shelby. *Liberating the Gospels: Reading the Bible with Jewish Eyes.* San Francisco: HarperSanFrancisco, 1997.

Stanton, Graham N. *A Gospel for a New People: Studies in Matthew.* Louisville, Ky.: Westminster/John Knox Press, 1992.

———. *Gospel Truth? New Light on Jesus and the Gospels.* Valley Forge, Pa.: Trinity Press International, 1995.

Wilson, A. N. *Jesus.* New York: W. W. Norton, 1992.

About SKYLIGHT PATHS Publishing

SkyLight Paths Publishing is creating a place where people of different spiritual traditions come together for challenge and inspiration, a place where we can help each other understand the mystery that lies at the heart of our existence.

Through spirituality, our religious beliefs are increasingly becoming a part of our lives—rather than *apart* from our lives. While many of us may be more interested than ever in spiritual growth, we may be less firmly planted in traditional religion. Yet, we do want to deepen our relationship to the sacred, to learn from our own as well as from other faith traditions, and to practice in new ways.

SkyLight Paths sees both believers and seekers as a community that increasingly transcends traditional boundaries of religion and denomination—people wanting to learn from each other, *walking together, finding the way.*

We at SkyLight Paths take great care to produce beautiful books that present meaningful spiritual content in a form that reflects the art of making high quality books. Therefore, we want to acknowledge those who contributed to the production of this book.

PRODUCTION
Jenny Buono & Tim Holtz

EDITORIAL
Sarah McBride, Maura D. Shaw & Emily Wichland

COVER DESIGN
Walter C. Bumford III, Stockton, Massachusetts

TEXT DESIGN
Chelsea Cloeter, River Forest, Illinois

PRINTING & BINDING
Versa Press, East Peoria, Illinois

AVAILABLE FROM BETTER BOOKSTORES.
TRY YOUR BOOKSTORE FIRST.

Other Interesting Books—Spirituality

Lighting the Lamp of Wisdom: *A Week Inside a Yoga Ashram*
by *John Ittner;* Foreword by *Dr. David Frawley*

This insider's guide to Hindu spiritual life takes you into a typical week of retreat inside a yoga ashram to demystify the experience and show you what to expect from your own visit. Includes a discussion of worship services, meditation and yoga classes, chanting and music, work practice, and more.
6 x 9, 192 pp, b/w photographs, Quality PB, ISBN 1-893361-52-7 **$15.95**; HC, ISBN 1-893361-37-3 **$24.95**

Waking Up: *A Week Inside a Zen Monastery*
by *Jack Maguire;* Foreword by *John Daido Loori, Roshi*

An essential guide to what it's like to spend a week inside a Zen Buddhist monastery.
6 x 9, 224 pp, b/w photographs, Quality PB, ISBN 1-893361-55-1 **$16.95**; HC, ISBN 1-893361-13-6 **$21.95**

Making a Heart for God: *A Week Inside a Catholic Monastery*
by *Dianne Aprile;* Foreword by *Brother Patrick Hart,* ocso

This essential guide to experiencing life in a Catholic monastery takes you to the Abbey of Gethsemani—the Trappist monastery in Kentucky that was home to author Thomas Merton—to explore the details. "More balanced and informative than the popular *The Cloister Walk* by Kathleen Norris." —*Choice: Current Reviews for Academic Libraries*
6 x 9, 224 pp, b/w photographs, Quality PB, ISBN 1-893361-49-7 **$16.95**; HC, ISBN 1-893361-14-4 **$21.95**

Come and Sit: *A Week Inside Meditation Centers*
by *Marcia Z. Nelson;* Foreword by *Wayne Teasdale*

The insider's guide to meditation in a variety of different spiritual traditions. Traveling through Buddhist, Hindu, Christian, Jewish, and Sufi traditions, this essential guide takes you to different meditation centers to meet the teachers and students and learn about the practices, demystifying the meditation experience.
6 x 9, 224 pp, b/w photographs, Quality PB, ISBN 1-893361-35-7 **$16.95**

Or phone, fax, mail or e-mail to: SKY**L**I**GHT** PATHS Publishing
Sunset Farm Offices, Route 4 • P.O. Box 237 • Woodstock, Vermont 05091
Tel: (802) 457-4000 • Fax: (802) 457-4004 • www.skylightpaths.com
Credit card orders: **(800) 962-4544** (8:30AM–5:30PM ET Monday–Friday)
Generous discounts on quantity orders. SATISFACTION GUARANTEED. Prices subject to change.

Spiritual Biography

The Life of Evelyn Underhill
An Intimate Portrait of the Groundbreaking Author of Mysticism
by *Margaret Cropper;* Foreword by *Dana Greene*

Evelyn Underhill was a passionate writer and teacher who wrote elegantly on mysticism, worship, and devotional life. This is the story of how she made her way toward spiritual maturity, from her early days of agnosticism to the years when her influence was felt throughout the world. 6 x 9, 288 pp, 5 b/w photos, Quality PB, ISBN 1-893361-70-5 **$18.95**

Zen Effects: *The Life of Alan Watts*
by *Monica Furlong*

The first and only full-length biography of one of the most charismatic spiritual leaders of the twentieth century—now back in print!

Through his widely popular books and lectures, Alan Watts (1915–1973) did more to introduce Eastern philosophy and religion to Western minds than any figure before or since. Here is the only biography of this charismatic figure, who served as Zen teacher, Anglican priest, lecturer, academic, entertainer, a leader of the San Francisco renaissance, and author of more than 30 books, including *The Way of Zen, Psychotherapy East and West* and *The Spirit of Zen.*
6 x 9, 264 pp, Quality PB, ISBN 1-893361-32-2 **$16.95**

   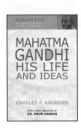

Simone Weil: *A Modern Pilgrimage*
by *Robert Coles*

The extraordinary life of the spiritual philosopher who's been called both saint and madwoman.

The French writer and philosopher Simone Weil (1906–1943) devoted her life to a search for God—while avoiding membership in organized religion. Robert Coles' intriguing study of Weil details her short, eventful life, and is an insightful portrait of the beloved and controversial thinker whose life and writings influenced many (from T. S. Eliot to Adrienne Rich to Albert Camus), and continue to inspire seekers everywhere. 6 x 9, 208 pp, Quality PB, ISBN 1-893361-34-9 **$16.95**

Mahatma Gandhi: *His Life and Ideas*
by *Charles F. Andrews;* Foreword by *Dr. Arun Gandhi*

An intimate biography of one of the greatest social and religious reformers of the modern world.

Examines from a contemporary Christian activist's point of view the religious ideas and political dynamics that influenced the birth of the peaceful resistance movement, the primary tool that Gandhi and the people of his homeland would use to gain India its freedom from British rule. An ideal introduction to the life and life's work of this great spiritual leader.
6 x 9, 336 pp, 5 b/w photos, Quality PB, ISBN 1-893361-89-6 **$18.95**

Spiritual Practice

The Sacred Art of Bowing
Preparing to Practice
by *Andi Young*

This informative and inspiring introduction to bowing—and related spiritual practices—shows you how to do it, why it's done, and what spiritual benefits it has to offer. Incorporates interviews, personal stories, illustrations of bowing in practice, advice on how you can incorporate bowing into your daily life, and how bowing can deepen spiritual understanding.
5½ x 8½, 128 pp, b/w illus., Quality PB, ISBN 1-893361-82-9 **$14.95**

Praying with Our Hands: *Twenty-One Practices of Embodied Prayer from the World's Spiritual Traditions*
by *Jon M. Sweeney;* Photographs by *Jennifer J. Wilson;*
Foreword by *Mother Tessa Bielecki;* Afterword by *Taitetsu Unno, PhD*

A spiritual guidebook for bringing prayer into our bodies.

This inspiring book of reflections and accompanying photographs shows us twenty-one simple ways of using our hands to speak to God, to enrich our devotion and ritual. All express the various approaches of the world's religious traditions to bringing the body into worship. Spiritual traditions represented include Anglican, Sufi, Zen, Roman Catholic, Yoga, Shaker, Hindu, Jewish, Pentecostal, Eastern Orthodox, and many others.
8 x 8, 96 pp, 22 duotone photographs, Quality PB, ISBN 1-893361-16-0 **$16.95**

  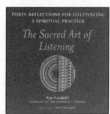 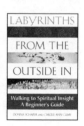

The Sacred Art of Listening
Forty Reflections for Cultivating a Spiritual Practice
by *Kay Lindahl;* Illustrations by *Amy Schnapper*

More than ever before, we need to embrace the skills and practice of listening. You will learn to: Speak clearly from your heart • Communicate with courage and compassion • Heighten your awareness for deep listening • Enhance your ability to listen to people with different belief systems. 8 x 8, 160 pp, Illus., Quality PB, ISBN 1-893361-44-6 **$16.99**

Labyrinths from the Outside In
Walking to Spiritual Insight—A Beginner's Guide
by *Donna Schaper* and *Carole Ann Camp*

The user-friendly, interfaith guide to making and using labyrinths—for meditation, prayer, and celebration.

Labyrinth walking is a spiritual exercise *anyone* can do. This accessible guide unlocks the mysteries of the labyrinth for all of us, providing ideas for using the labyrinth walk for prayer, meditation, and celebrations to mark the most important moments in life. Includes instructions for making a labyrinth of your own and finding one in your area.
6 x 9, 208 pp, b/w illus. and photographs, Quality PB, ISBN 1-893361-18-7 **$16.95**

SkyLight Illuminations Series
Andrew Harvey, series editor

Offers today's spiritual seeker an enjoyable entry into the great classic texts of the world's spiritual traditions. Each classic is presented in an accessible translation, with facing pages of guided commentary from experts, giving you the keys you need to understand the history, context, and meaning of the text. This series enables readers of all backgrounds to experience and understand classic spiritual texts directly, and to make them a part of their lives. Andrew Harvey writes the foreword to each volume, an insightful, personal introduction to each classic.

Bhagavad Gita: *Annotated & Explained*
Translation by *Shri Purohit Swami*; Annotation by *Kendra Crossen Burroughs*

"The very best Gita for first-time readers." —Ken Wilber

Millions of people turn daily to India's most beloved holy book, whose universal appeal has made it popular with non-Hindus and Hindus alike. This edition introduces you to the characters, explains references and philosophical terms, shares the interpretations of famous spiritual leaders and scholars, and more. 5½ x 8½, 192 pp, Quality PB, ISBN 1-893361-28-4 **$16.95**

  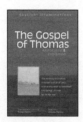 

The Way of a Pilgrim: *Annotated & Explained*
Translation and annotation by *Gleb Pokrovsky*

This classic of Russian spirituality is the delightful account of one man who sets out to learn the prayer of the heart—also known as the "Jesus prayer"—and how the practice transforms his life. 5½ x 8½, 160 pp, Illus., Quality PB, ISBN 1-893361-31-4 **$14.95**

The Gospel of Thomas: *Annotated & Explained*
Translation and annotation by *Stevan Davies*

Discovered in 1945, this collection of aphoristic sayings sheds new light on the origins of Christianity and the intriguing figure of Jesus, portraying the Kingdom of God as a present fact about the world, rather than a future promise or future threat. This edition guides you through the text with annotations that focus on the meaning of the sayings. 5½ x 8½, 192 pp, Quality PB, ISBN 1-893361-45-4 **$16.95**

Rumi and Islam: *Selections from His Stories, Poems, and Discourses—Annotated & Explained*
Translation and annotation by *Ibrahim Gamard*

Offers a new way of thinking about Rumi's poetry. Ibrahim Gamard focuses on Rumi's place within the Sufi tradition of Islam, providing you with insight into the mystical side of the religion—one that has love of God at its core and sublime wisdom teachings as its pathways. 5½ x 8½, 240 pp, Quality PB, ISBN 1-59473-002-4 **$15.99**

SkyLight Illuminations Series
Andrew Harvey, series editor

Zohar: *Annotated & Explained*
Translation and annotation by *Daniel C. Matt*

The cornerstone text of Kabbalah.

The best-selling author of *The Essential Kabbalah* brings together in one place the most important teachings of the *Zohar*, the canonical text of Jewish mystical tradition. Guides you step by step through the midrash, mystical fantasy, and Hebrew scripture that make up the *Zohar*, explaining the inner meanings in facing-page commentary. Ideal for readers without any prior knowledge of Jewish mysticism.

5½ x 8½, 176 pp, Quality PB, ISBN 1-893361-51-9 **$15.99**

Selections from the Gospel of Sri Ramakrishna
Annotated & Explained
Translation by *Swami Nikhilananda*; Annotation by *Kendra Crossen Burroughs*

The words of India's greatest example of God-consciousness and mystical ecstasy in recent history.

Introduces the fascinating world of the Indian mystic and the universal appeal of his message that has inspired millions of devotees for more than a century. Selections from the original text and insightful yet unobtrusive commentary highlight the most important and inspirational teachings. Ideal for readers without any prior knowledge of Hinduism.

5½ x 8½, 240 pp, b/w photographs, Quality PB, ISBN 1-893361-46-2 **$16.95**

Dhammapada: *Annotated & Explained*
Translation by *Max Müller* and revised by *Jack Maguire*; Annotation by *Jack Maguire*

The classic of Buddhist spiritual practice.

The Dhammapada—words spoken by the Buddha himself over 2,500 years ago—is notoriously difficult to understand for the first-time reader. Now you can experience it with understanding even if you have no previous knowledge of Buddhism. Enlightening facing-page commentary explains all the names, terms, and references, giving you deeper insight into the text.

5½ x 8½, 160 pp, b/w photographs, Quality PB, ISBN 1-893361-42-X **$14.95**

Hasidic Tales: *Annotated & Explained*
Translation and annotation by *Rabbi Rami Shapiro*

The legendary tales of the impassioned Hasidic rabbis.

The allegorical quality of Hasidic tales can be perplexing. Here, they are presented as stories rather than parables, making them accessible and meaningful. Each demonstrates the spiritual power of unabashed joy, offers lessons for leading a holy life, and reminds us that the Divine can be found in the everyday. Annotations explain theological concepts, introduce major characters, and clarify references unfamiliar to most readers.

5½ x 8½, 240 pp, Quality PB, ISBN 1-893361-86-1 **$16.95**

Meditation/Prayer

Finding Grace at the Center: *The Beginning of Centering Prayer*
by *M. Basil Pennington, OCSO, Thomas Keating, OCSO,* and *Thomas E. Clarke, SJ*
The book that helped launch the Centering Prayer "movement." Explains the prayer of *The Cloud of Unknowing,* posture and relaxation, the three simple rules of centering prayer, and how to cultivate centering prayer throughout all aspects of your life.
5 x 7¼, 112 pp, HC, ISBN 1-893361-69-1 **$14.95**

Prayers to an Evolutionary God
by *William Cleary;* Afterword by *Diarmuid O'Murchu*
How is it possible to pray when God is dislocated from heaven, dispersed all around us, and more of a creative force than an all-knowing father? In this unique collection of eighty prose prayers and related commentary, William Cleary considers new ways of thinking about God and the world around us. Inspired by the spiritual and scientific teachings of Diarmuid O'Murchu and Teilhard de Chardin, Cleary reveals that religion and science can be combined to create an expanding view of the universe—an evolutionary faith.
6 x 9, 208 pp, HC, ISBN 1-59473-006-7 **$21.99**

 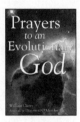 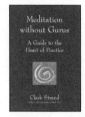 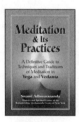

Meditation without Gurus
A Guide to the Heart of Practice
by *Clark Strand*
Short, compelling reflections show you how to make meditation a part of your daily life, without the complication of gurus, mantras, retreats, or treks to distant mountains. This enlightening book strips the practice down to its essential heart—simplicity, lightness, and peace—showing you that the most important part of practice is not whether you can get in the full lotus position, but rather your ability to become fully present in the moment.
5½ x 8½, 192 pp, Quality PB, ISBN 1-893361-93-4 **$16.95**

Meditation & Its Practices
A Definitive Guide to Techniques and Traditions of Meditation in Yoga and Vedanta
by *Swami Adiswarananda*

The complete sourcebook for exploring Hinduism's two most time-honored traditions of meditation.

Drawing on both classic and contemporary sources, this comprehensive sourcebook outlines the scientific, psychological, and spiritual elements of Yoga and Vedanta meditation.
6 x 9, 504 pp, HC, ISBN 1-893361-83-7 **$34.95**

Children's Spirituality

ENDORSED BY CATHOLIC, PROTESTANT, JEWISH, AND BUDDHIST RELIGIOUS LEADERS

Becoming Me: *A Story of Creation*
by *Martin Boroson*
Full-color illus. by *Christopher Gilvan-Cartwright*

For ages 4 & up

Told in the personal "voice" of the Creator, here is a story about creation and relationship that is about each one of us. In simple words and with radiant illustrations, the Creator tells an intimate story about love, about friendship and playing, about our world—and about ourselves. And with each turn of the page, we're reminded that we just might be closer to our Creator than we think!

8 x 10, 32 pp, Full-color illus., HC, ISBN 1-893361-11-X **$16.95**

Noah's Wife
The Story of Naamah
by *Sandy Eisenberg Sasso*
Full-color illus. by *Bethanne Andersen*

For ages 4 & up

This new story, based on an ancient text, opens readers' religious imaginations to new ideas about the well-known story of the Flood. When God tells Noah to bring the animals of the world onto the ark, God also calls on Naamah, Noah's wife, to save each plant on Earth. "A lovely tale.... Children of all ages should be drawn to this parable for our times."
—Tomie de Paola, artist/author of books for children
9 x 12, 32 pp, HC, Full-color illus., ISBN 1-58023-134-9 **$16.95**

In God's Name
by *Sandy Eisenberg Sasso;* Full-color illus. by *Phoebe Stone*

For ages 4 & up

Like an ancient myth in its poetic text and vibrant illustrations, this award-winning modern fable about the search for God's name celebrates the diversity and, at the same time, the unity of all the people of the world.
9 x 12, 32 pp, HC, Full-color illus., ISBN 1-879045-26-5 **$16.95**

Also available in Spanish:
El nombre de Dios 9 x 12, 32 pp, HC, Full-color illus., ISBN 1-893361-63-2 **$16.95**

The 11th Commandment
Wisdom from Our Children
by *The Children of America*

For ages 4 & up

"If there were an Eleventh Commandment, what would it be?" Children of many religious denominations across America answer this question—in their own drawings and words. "A rare book of spiritual celebration for all people, of all ages, for all time." —*Bookviews*
8 x 10, 48 pp, HC, Full-color illus., ISBN 1-879045-46-X **$16.95**

Children's Spirituality

ENDORSED BY CATHOLIC, PROTESTANT, JEWISH, AND BUDDHIST RELIGIOUS LEADERS

Because Nothing Looks Like God

by *Lawrence and Karen Kushner*
Full-color illus. by
Dawn W. Majewski

For ages 4 & up

MULTICULTURAL, NONDENOMINATIONAL, NONSECTARIAN

Real-life examples of happiness and sadness—from goodnight stories, to the hope and fear felt the first time at bat, to the closing moments of life—introduce children to the possibilities of spiritual life. A vibrant way for children—and their adults—to explore what, where, and how God is in our lives.

11 x 8½, 32 pp, HC, Full-color illus., ISBN 1-58023-092-X **$16.95**

Also available: **Teacher's Guide,** 8½ x 11, 22 pp, PB, ISBN 1-58023-140-3 **$6.95** For ages 5–8

Where Is God? (A Board Book)

For ages 0–4

by *Lawrence and Karen Kushner*; Full-color illus. by *Dawn W. Majewski*

A gentle way for young children to explore how God is with us every day, in every way. Abridged from *Because Nothing Looks Like God* by Lawrence and Karen Kushner and specially adapted to board book format to delight and inspire young readers.

5 x 5, 24 pp, Board, Full-color illus., ISBN 1-893361-17-9 **$7.95**

What Does God Look Like? (A Board Book)

For ages 0–4

by *Lawrence and Karen Kushner*; Full-color illus. by *Dawn W. Majewski*

A simple way for young children to explore the ways that we "see" God. Abridged from *Because Nothing Looks Like God* by Lawrence and Karen Kushner and specially adapted to board book format to delight and inspire young readers.

5 x 5, 24 pp, Board, Full-color illus., ISBN 1-893361-23-3 **$7.95**

How Does God Make Things Happen? (A Board Book)

For ages 0–4

by *Lawrence and Karen Kushner*; Full-color illus. by *Dawn W. Majewski*

A charming invitation for young children to explore how God makes things happen in our world. Abridged from *Because Nothing Looks Like God* by Lawrence and Karen Kushner and specially adapted to board book format to delight and inspire young readers.

5 x 5, 24 pp, Board, Full-color illus., ISBN 1-893361-24-1 **$7.95**

What Is God's Name? (A Board Book)

For ages 0–4

by *Sandy Eisenberg Sasso*; Full-color illus. by *Phoebe Stone*

Everyone and everything in the world has a name. What is God's name? Abridged from the award-winning *In God's Name* by Sandy Eisenberg Sasso and specially adapted to board book format to delight and inspire young readers.

5 x 5, 24 pp, Board, Full-color illus., ISBN 1-893361-10-1 **$7.95**

Children's Spiritual Biography

MULTICULTURAL, NONDENOMINATIONAL, NONSECTARIAN

Ten Amazing People
And How They Changed the World
by *Maura D. Shaw*; Foreword by *Dr. Robert Coles*
Full-color illus. by *Stephen Marchesi*

> For ages 7 & up

Black Elk • Dorothy Day • Malcolm X • Mahatma Gandhi • Martin Luther King, Jr. • Mother Teresa • Janusz Korczak • Desmond Tutu • Thich Nhat Hanh • Albert Schweitzer

This vivid, inspirational, and authoritative book will open new possibilities for children by telling the stories of how ten of the past century's greatest leaders changed the world in important ways.

8½ x 11, 48 pp, HC, Full-color illus., ISBN 1-893361-47-0 **$17.95**

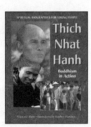

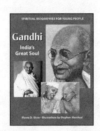

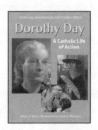

A new series: Spiritual Biographies for Young People

Thich Nhat Hanh: *Buddhism in Action*

> For ages 7 & up

by *Maura D. Shaw*; Full-color illus. by *Stephen Marchesi*

Warm illustrations, photos, age-appropriate activities, and Thich Nhat Hanh's own poems introduce a great man to children in a way they can understand and enjoy. Includes a list of important Buddhist words to know.

6¾ x 8¾, 32 pp, HC, Full-color illus., ISBN 1-893361-87-X **$12.95**

Gandhi: *India's Great Soul*

> For ages 7 & up

by *Maura D. Shaw*; Full-color illus. by *Stephen Marchesi*

There are a number of biographies of Gandhi written for young readers, but this is the only one that balances a simple text with illustrations, photographs, and activities that encourage children and adults to talk about how to make changes happen without violence. Introduces children to important concepts of freedom, equality, and justice among people of all backgrounds and religions.

6¾ x 8¾, 32 pp, HC, Full-color illus., ISBN 1-893361-91-8 **$12.95**

Dorothy Day: *A Catholic Life of Action*

> For ages 7 & up

by *Maura D. Shaw*; Full-color illus. by *Stephen Marchesi*

Introduces children to one of the most inspiring women of the twentieth century, a down-to-earth spiritual leader who saw the presence of God in every person she met. Includes practical activities, a timeline, and a list of important words to know.

6¾ x 8¾, 32 pp, HC, Full-color illus., ISBN 1-59473-011-3 **$12.99**

Interspirituality

A Walk with Four Spiritual Guides
Krishna, Buddha, Jesus, and Ramakrishna
by *Andrew Harvey*

> Andrew Harvey's warm and personal introduction to each guide offers his own experiences of learning from their wisdom.

Krishna, Buddha, Jesus, Ramakrishna: four of the world's most interesting and challenging spiritual masters. The core of their most important teachings—along with annotations from expert scholars and introductions from Andrew Harvey, one of the great spiritual thinkers of our time—now are all in one beautiful volume.

5½ x 8½, 192 pp, 10 b/w photos & illus., Hardcover, ISBN 1-893361-73-X **$21.95**

The Alphabet of Paradise: *An A–Z of Spirituality for Everyday Life*
by *Howard Cooper*

"An extraordinary book." —Karen Armstrong

One of the most eloquent new voices in spirituality, Howard Cooper takes us on a journey of discovery—into ourselves and into the past—to find the signposts that can help us live more meaningful lives. In twenty-six engaging chapters—from A to Z—Cooper spiritually illuminates the subjects of daily life, using an ancient Jewish mystical method of interpretation that reveals both the literal and more allusive meanings of each. Topics include: Awe, Bodies, Creativity, Dreams, Emotions, Sports, and more.

5 x 7¾, 224 pp, Quality PB, ISBN 1-893361-80-2 **$16.95**

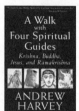  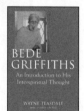 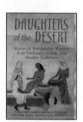

Daughters of the Desert: *Tales of Remarkable Women from Christian, Jewish, and Muslim Traditions*
by *Claire Rudolf Murphy, Meghan Nuttall Sayres, Mary Cronk Farrell, Sarah Conover,* and *Betsy Wharton*

Breathes new life into the old tales of our female ancestors in faith.

The authors use traditional scriptural passages as their starting points, then with vivid detail fill in historical context and place. Chapters reveal the voices of Sarah, Hagar, Huldah, Esther, Salome, Mary Magdalene, Lydia, Khadija, Fatima, and many more. Historical fiction ideal for readers of all ages. 5½ x 8½, 192 pp, HC, ISBN 1-893361-72-1 **$19.95**

Bede Griffiths: *An Introduction to His Interspiritual Thought*
by *Wayne Teasdale*

The first in-depth study of Bede Griffiths' contemplative experience and thought.

Wayne Teasdale, a longtime personal friend and student of Griffiths, creates in this intimate portrait an intriguing view into the beliefs and life of this champion of interreligious acceptance and harmony. Explains key terms that form the basis of Griffiths' contemplative understanding, and the essential characteristics of his theology as they relate to the Hindu and Christian traditions.

6 x 9, 288 pp, Quality PB, ISBN 1-893361-77-2 **$18.95**